MARKETING AI™

FROM AUTOMATION TO REVENUE PERFORMANCE MARKETING

Greg Grdodian and Stevan Roberts

ISBN-13: 9780692602287
ISBN-10: 0692602283
Library of Congress Control Number: 2015921035
Reach Marketing LLC, Pearl River, NY

Dedication

My mother, Ann Grdodian, taught me that nothing is impossible; my wife Diane and daughters, Nadia and Ava, inspire me and fuel my desire to succeed; my cousin, Vahe Barsoian, taught me to put others first; and my dear friend Stevan Roberts taught me to love what I do. This book is dedicated to them, the most instrumental people in my personal and professional life.

—Greg Grdodian

*To my darling wife, Michelle, whose love and support mean the world to me,
and to my children, William and Jonathan, who inspire me to learn new things
every day, and to Edith Roman, my mentor in business and life.*

— Stevan Roberts

About the Authors

Stevan Roberts, Chairman, Reach Marketing

Stevan Roberts brings more than 30 years of executive experience to his role as chairman at Reach Marketing. Most recently, he was chief executive officer of InfoGroup subsidiary Edith Roman Associates. Under Roberts' leadership the company pioneered innovative customer acquisition, retention tools, and marketing strategies. Roberts revolutionized the way businesses effectively and affordably build relationships with their customers, and how they attract and retain new clients.

Roberts is a veteran technology and marketing innovator with extensive experience in database, automation, network applications, and end-user implementation. He was CEO of Database Direct and ePost-Direct, pioneers in the database, business content, email list, and email deployment industries.

Roberts has contributed to evolving industry standards and has presented information and strategies at major industry conferences, contributes articles to trade publications, and co-authored *Internet Direct Mail: The Complete Guide to Successful E-Mail Marketing Campaigns.*

Greg Grdodian, CEO, Reach Marketing

Greg Grdodian is the innovation and creative leader at Reach Marketing, where he built, conceptualized, and developed a suite of integrated marketing services for the company's clients. He devoted the first 16 years of his professional career to InfoGroup/Edith Roman, rising to the position of president in 2010, and while there developed industry-leading multi-channel products and tactics. He then joined Crain Communications as director of audience development and established revenue performance marketing strategies that tripled growth by optimizing digital products and services for this world-renowned media firm.

Grdodian's experience covers a broad spectrum of extract, transform, and load technologies, and audience, content development, customer identification, and database marketing automation technologies. He pioneered the Marketing AI™ system to build an autonomous omni-channel capability for Reach's revenue performance marketing services group.

Reach Marketing LLC

Reach Marketing is a revenue performance marketing firm that develops innovative, integrated marketing solutions that help businesses engage their target audiences more effectively and quickly grow their sales through synergistic omni-channel marketing.

The company was launched by Stevan Roberts, Wayne Roberts, Greg Grdodian, and Chris Longo, the former marketing-management and technology team at Edith Roman Associates. Based in Pearl River, NY, Reach comprises service-oriented professionals who are passionate about bringing innovative marketing solutions to their B2B and B2C clients. Services include marketing automation, database management, email marketing, inbound lead generation, list brokerage, list management, data hygiene, data and email append, SEO, and social media.

Reach Marketing is the only company that brings together an interdisciplinary team of IT, software development, marketing, audience development, database marketing, analytics, SEO/SMO, and digital experts within one organization to drive the success of its clients.

PROLOGUE

I f you're not looking to the future of your business, it will be left in the past.

Marketing AI: From Automation to Revenue Performance Marketing is more than a book. It's a key — the key to your company's sustainable success. The doors it unlocks lead directly to high-value site traffic, increased quality leads, deeper insight into your customers, and sales revenue growth. Marketers will learn how to get the right message to the right individual at the right time, every time, and they'll do it with far less effort than they may have thought. The reason? They have a powerful ally: Marketing Artificial Intelligence (MAI).

When we talk about artificial intelligence, we refer to two of its facets. First, marketing automation has the capacity to learn and evolve within its marketing framework, making it an "intelligent" system. This progressive learning finely tunes each marketing campaign more than the last as the software and its users turn behavioral feedback into instructions for the next campaign. Second, *intelligence* refers to the knowledge itself: Think of the phrase *military intelligence,* meaning information that is gathered and studied to help guide military decision-makers. It's vital information.

Automation is at the forefront of a movement toward assisted intelligence that boosts the interactivity between human ingenuity and software. Marketing AI transforms your marketing from an art into a science through a process of automation. With marketing automation you get the steady, quantifiable metrics that make sales and marketing systematic instead of random. It offers four advantages that traditional marketing software lacks: scalability, predictability, reproducibility, and sustainability.

An AI able to work with its operators, adapt itself to an environment, and learn how to do its job better over time is already here, and it's where marketing automation is now. If synchronized and executed properly, there's no doubt that the combination of human ingenuity and automated precision represents a huge leap forward.

Each buyer is unique, as is each buyer's journey. You can accompany buyers on these journeys, but you can't be there for every individual buyer unless you have a way of being in many places at once. Your Marketing AI is the way to "be" with all your potential buyers: It takes over routine operations, intuiting what your prospects need and delivers the information they want when they want it. We see a marketing future that relies on Marketing AI to personalize marketing campaigns for an infinite number of customer journeys.

The following questions may seem elementary but the answers are not simple. Do you know your customers — really know them, beyond their names, and billing and shipping addresses? Do you know how they interact with your site, your content, and your product or service? Knowing who your customers are and how they found you; why they *are* your customers; how they interact with your site, your content, and your product; and how to find more like them requires having more data about them, plus the tools to interpret that data. You need to gain this knowledge, whether directly from your customers, through data appends, or by observing it from behavioral cues. The information you gather creates a complete picture of your customers.

Data needs context to be meaningful, though, and it's a challenge to make sense of all the information coming to you. To meet that challenge, you need to have a mind like a computer or a computer that thinks like the human mind — an artificial intelligence.

The Turing Test

In the mid-1940s British computing scientist and mathematician Alan M. Turing attempted to codify a method by which we recognize the way machines "learn." Turing's posit about AI — that a computer would deserve to be called intelligent if it could deceive a human into believing that it was human — led him to suggest a test for a machine's ability to behave, or "think," like a human.

The Turing Test is the benchmark of a true AI; a single system has yet to pass it completely, partially because of the way that machines learn. The reinforcement learning that intelligent systems undergo is inspired by how *we* learn, but it isn't an identical process. Rather, it's the synergy of an automated system working in concert with human ingenuity.

In today's highly evolved marketing world, AI has moved beyond Turing's idea into a digital arena where a complete, intelligent, integrated process unifies the symbiosis between sales and marketing.

From Marketing Automation to Marketing AI

Much of human history has been about developing better and more efficient tools. AI is designed to do the same thing for the mind that tools do for the body, improving our ability to see relationships, coordinate communications, spot opportunities, and assess risks. Marketing automation acts as such an effective force multiplier for your marketing efforts that it's useful to look at the combination of your marketing team's ingenuity and a marketing automation system (MAS) as the first steps toward a complete AI.

Marketing AI perceives its environment and automatically triggers actions that maximize your company's best chances for success. Marketing automation provides you with a complete, integrated, intelligent user interface that unifies your marketing, from lead generation to content coordination to analytics. It nurtures your prospects with the right information delivered at the right time and increases the speed at which qualified prospects convert into profitable customers. Implemented correctly, your Marketing AI adapts and creates ever-improving revenue performance by learning the processes, campaigns, content channels, and timing that increase success.

In the past it would have been impossible to know the sequence or combination of marketing materials that successfully converted a prospect into a customer. The Internet has provided a critical intelligence capability that allows computers to track and analyze both anonymous and known prospects' behavior — how they found your company, the web pages they're viewing, what's resonating and what they respond to — even before your sales team knows its leads' names. The data that your AI uses to gain knowledge comes in at lightning-fast speed, and it goes through the process far more quickly than any human mind can.

The Evolution of Marketing

In the early days of marketing, prospective customers first learned about your product or service through separate, often disjointed campaigns that included space advertising, direct mail, TV, and outbound telemarketing campaigns. Once a prospect became interested, it was the job of the sales team to explain the benefits and differentiate the brand enough to make a sale. Sellers learned through trial and error which responses to different sales situations produced the best results. The human mind is very good at such adaptations, but even the best brains in the business couldn't accurately correlate information about customers' behavior and demographic data with marketing techniques. To do that required a technological leap forward.

Sales and marketing departments have also undergone a huge shift in how much information they have to manage. What may have been possible when a business received a handful of sales leads each day is no longer viable, because companies process thousands or even hundreds of thousands of buy signals each day — many times faster than the organization sales teams can adapt to. As a result, sales and marketing teams have become overloaded.

The information revolution made sweeping changes to countless industries, but few have been as completely transformed as marketing. Instead of the top-down, one-way model of communication with almost no visible feedback from customers that was the marketing model for decades, businesses are now in constant connection with their prospects and customers. Maintaining that connection and guiding conversation have become the challenges of 21st-century marketing.

This revolution is comparable to a previous seismic shift that happened more than half a century ago when advertisers made the move from radio to television. Suddenly, getting your message across was more than just a matter of making it sound good; it also had to look good. This new dimension revolutionized how companies marketed themselves and their products, and by extension it changed how marketing companies operated.

The old top-down concept of marketing to a largely silent, uninvolved audience is as outmoded as radio jingles became in the age of television. Today, marketing's new dimension is in a virtual realm, and it's as reliant on technology as it is on creative. Technology has opened up new marketing channels via email, SEO, social media networks, blogs, video, and other content.

It can also give marketers a panoramic view of an industry using big data and analytics that make sense of it. Being able to scan the entirety of a market, create customer profiles to discover who your audience is, identify prospects with the greatest potential, draw a marketing blueprint, execute your plan, and analyze the data from every campaign holds the key to your organization's stability and growth. To accomplish this, you need both creative vision and the technology to implement it.

A Marketing AI Blueprint

Implementing marketing automation is the key to every phase of the marketing cycle, from discovery through execution and analysis. Many companies offer automation software, but there's a huge difference between installing automation software and creating a reliable Marketing AI. In this book, we explain how you can combine central intelligence, best practices, modern marketing channels, and automation strategies with Marketing AI to produce a winning marketing program — your marketing AI blueprint.

The Marketing Lead Lifecycle

The marketing Lead Lifecycle (Figure P1), sometimes referred to as the sales funnel, is the grand, unified theory of contemporary marketing and is guided and tracked at every step by your Marketing AI. It's the stage that each lead enters, from the moment it begins to interact with you until the deal is closed. But the Lead Lifecycle concept doesn't exist in a vacuum: It's linked to your content development, your leads' sales readiness, and your nurture campaigns. It connects every aspect of your marketing efforts into one cohesive process that from the outset adapts and responds to improve the conversion of a lead from prospect to customer.

We discuss every phase of your marketing funnel in detail throughout *Marketing AI: From Automation to Revenue Performance Marketing*, but this overarching cycle of lead development is an element that you'll see again and again. With it, you already have the outline of a superior marketing strategy, and you'll learn how to implement and execute this strategy flawlessly. And because your sales funnel doesn't operate in a vacuum, you'll also gain insight into what your Marketing AI can do for

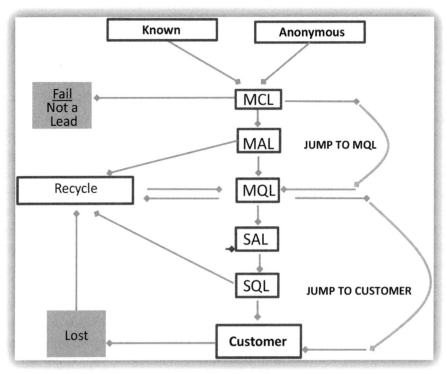

The Lead Lifecycle

you *before and after* your prospects' trip through the funnel. With that knowledge, you'll be able to guide their trajectories on all their buying journeys.

There are three phases — discovery, execution, and analysis — that comprise the Lead Lifecycle.

Discovery

Before you can reach your customers and guide their path through your sales funnel, you need to know who they are. Creating a central intelligence alignment is key here because the discovery phase is largely data-driven, and your MAS excels at dealing with data and at streamlining the discovery process. It's the "who" and "what" of marketing, the beginning of a buyer's journey and the earliest information that your AI processes. With your Marketing AI, your data-science team can dig deep into the numbers that represent your audience and the budget you're allocating to reach it. This initial step includes data normalization (to standardize all your data fields, values, and elements); data hygiene (to identify and purge inactive records); data integrity (to lend depth to raw numbers and create a more realistic image of your ideal customer base); and enhancement (to define your audience more precisely).

Even though marketers acknowledge the importance of discovery, most of them view it as dull housekeeping. Fortunately, marketing automation software does most of the heavy lifting, removing routine tasks from the discovery process. Discovery translates directly into improving your relevance, and relevance is critical to your marketing efforts, especially when you're reaching your audience digitally. You can't be relevant to your audience until you understand its needs, and that starts with effective profiling. The discovery process helps crystallize your knowledge of your audience so that you can communicate your benefits to it. Along the way, you'll also uncover important details about your own strategy. Defining your goals with the campaign is essential to your marketing and technology teams as you move to the next phase of your marketing plan.

Once you know more about your audience through demographic, firmographic, behavioral, and contextual data, marketing specialists and data scientists work together within your Marketing AI to design and build your marketing strategy's infrastructure. Many marketing departments want to rush headlong to this phase, thinking it's where the fun begins, but without the essential analytics from the early discovery phase, no creative push you make will have much impact. This is where your Marketing AI truly shines, because it lets you move the building blocks of your campaign around to construct a sturdy framework for success.

The early steps of the discovery phase tells you who you want to reach and how you want to connect; the later stages are a blueprint that outlines precisely how you'll get there. Automation lets you define every part of your blueprint with customizable flows that guide prospects through your marketing pipeline. After you have your plan, it's time to put it into action.

Execution

Even the best planning won't mean a thing if your execution doesn't produce the right content for the right person at the right time. Your technology and data scientists have done their work, and in the execution phase, creative takes over and shines. Your content creation team produces compelling content, and your MAS routes it to where it needs to go and gathers behavioral feedback on how your audience interacts with it. Different content streams go to different leads at different phases of their buying journeys in a dance so complex, you need a Marketing AI to coordinate its steps.

Building solid landing pages, developing your SEO, coming up with outstanding email creative and compelling copy are all key parts of execution, and you'll learn extensive process details about each of these elements. Is no one opening your email or reading your blog? Are you getting too little traffic for the amount of time and effort you've invested in SEO? What are the differences between web-based content and print media? How do social networks fit with your marketing plan? These are some of the questions your marketing team needs to answer and correct to see growth.

Analysis

Every campaign generates data, and data is incredibly valuable. With it, you can achieve greater relevance to your audience, expand your brand, and save money by cutting what doesn't work.

You can cross- and upsell more effectively with deeper analysis. Attribution shows data analysts where your traffic is really coming from and where it's going, and marketing automation plays an essential role in it. This phase is the last step in the previous marketing campaign's lifecycle, and it also transitions seamlessly into the first step of your next campaign, generating data you can then use to improve your discovery process.

A Marketing AI Mind Map

Content and data that are isolated from each other will lack relevance. Only when brilliant creative and mountains of data come together with the technology to make sense of that data and sharpen your creative edge do you get the kind of marketing that works in a modern context. We've developed a way to preplan your strategy while fusing creative and technology into a whole that's greater than the sum of its parts.

Marketing AI: From Automation to Revenue Performance Marketing is your mind map of a comprehensive Marketing AI, one that takes full advantage of the forward leap into digital media and prepares you for the next generation of technology while delivering results today. You'll learn much more about what marketing automation is, what it isn't, and where it fits into a marketing strategy. You'll also discover more about traditional marketing through the lens of automation and read a compelling case study about how one company went from finding itself in a marketing dead zone to flourishing as an automated, intelligent, and responsive organization that converted its old marketing plan into a revenue marketing strategy.

CONTENTS

PART I

MARKETING AUTOMATION:
SETTING THE STAGE

CHAPTER 1

WHAT IS MARKETING AUTOMATION?

Marketing automation is where data, content, and state-of-the-art technology meet, and investing in the right marketing tools now will mean the difference between leading your industry and being just another follower. There are many different marketing automation options, each of which has its strengths. Choosing the right marketing strategy is critical, and knowing as much as possible about your best options is essential to making that decision. Let's look at what each of these systems must have to give you what you need.

A well-designed system captures leads, scores those leads to indicate where your best prospects are, streamlines content creation, handles omni-channel content coordination, develops marketing flows to lead buyers through their decision-making process, and analyzes data. You can find separate software that accomplishes some of these same tasks, but those tools don't communicate with one another. They can't give you the big-picture view that automation can. It's important to note that omni-channel marketing is not the same as multichannel marketing. Omni-channel is a multichannel approach to marketing that focuses on engaging with each customer or prospect through multiple marketing channels with a single voice to maximize recall and eventual conversion. It implies having complete knowledge of the ways all your marketing efforts perform and how that information will guide future business decisions.

Marketing AI gives you benefits — scalability, predictability, reproducibility, and sustainability (SPRS) — that no other marketing system does.

Scalability

Marketing automation software offers full scalability, whether you're working with an audience size of a few thousand leads or a few million. That's important — even to smaller businesses, because successful small businesses won't stay small forever. Your customers win, too, with a fully scalable system, because they get the attention they deserve, making your lead nurture program vastly more effective than it would be with conventional marketing techniques.

The term *sales pipeline* is often used to describe how prospects flow in at one end of the funnel and move through the process, picking up more information and getting more input that helps them make a buying decision. Like an actual pipeline, the conventional marketing pipeline can only handle a certain volume. Too much traffic, and would-be customers no longer get the information they need. These potential customers leak out of the pipeline because they aren't nurtured with a steady feed of information.

Automation turns a narrow, restrictive pipeline into a flexible, responsive pathway that accommodates as many customers as you feed into it. The same flow moves through your marketing funnel regardless of its volume, ensuring that the system grows with the company using it. Scalability is a must for revenue marketing. A smaller firm that outgrows its marketing strategy often loses what made it successful. But with an integrated, scalable automated system, it continues its initial success into the future.

Predictability

Marketing automation systems (MASs) deal in big data, crunching numbers that no single person or even team of data scientists could handle. Scientists use tools to manage and analyze huge volumes of data for everything from discovering new planetary systems to unraveling the human genome. Big data applications excel at predictive power, too, and that's where these applications become especially interesting to marketers. Knowing where your customers are is important but being able to assess where they'll be in the future is even more vital.

When a system has great predictive power, it also has greater predictability. You get the results you expect to get, and you can rely on your data to create a true picture of your customer base, your campaigns' effectiveness, and your leads' sales readiness.

Marketing automation allows exponentially greater predictability of everything from lead acquisition and lead nurturing to customer retention. Lead ranking and management tools let marketing automation software accurately predict how many leads will flow into each part of your sales pipeline and when these leads reach a new level of sales-readiness. By knowing how many leads your marketing team must generate and nurture to reach a given revenue target, you have the knowledge you need to prepare for future growth.

Reproducibility

Reproducible testing results are a cornerstone of scientific inquiry. A few years ago, cold fusion had the world excited, but not for long. The anomalous testing results that the initial team achieved couldn't be repeated, and without reproducible results, it just wasn't science. Automation turns raw data into the science of marketing by reliably producing expected results.

A single success might as well be luck. With the reproducibility of marketing automation, you have sustainable growth. The software works not just with a single campaign, but also with every successive campaign, forming a comprehensive marketing strategy designed to boost revenue while serving your leads and customers what they need to make key buying decisions. Until you can pinpoint why a campaign was a success or why it fell short, you can neither excel in future campaigns nor protect yourself from costly failures.

Sustainability

Scalability, predictability, and reproducibility are meaningless without the continued ability to find new leads and new markets. Products and services go through lifecycles. In the early stages, the market of early adopters keeps your target narrow and focused. As the product or service is more widely accepted, the market will explode with an ever-increasing need to separate the wheat from the chaff. In the mature stage, the market will become commoditized, requiring you to nurture and mine every qualified lead. Markets aren't infinite, so your growth strategy needs to be able to adapt to changes in the marketplace. Your market will inevitably drift, reach plateaus, or shift in response to competitors. Marketing automation allows a growth-oriented marketing strategy in a new market to evolve into relationship building in a maturing market and to seek new ways to add value to an established one. The marketing messages you send to grow a market are very different from those you give your prospects when you're nurturing an existing audience or expanding in an entirely different direction. With marketing automation, your Marketing AI will be able to recycle and nurture every lead and identify marketing trends and new sectors of profitability that will sustain your business and allow you to outmaneuver your competition.

The Fifth Element: Velocity

Scalability, predictability, reproducibility, and sustainability contribute to a crucial fifth aspect of marketing automation: velocity. The speed at which your prospects move through your marketing funnel dictates how many sales you make, how much time your sales and marketing teams invest in leads, and how you manage increases in lead volume. All four elements of the SPRS formula affect velocity, and all four are equally important aspects of a complete system. We'll talk more about velocity Chapter 4, when we dig deeper into big data.

What Marketing Automation Isn't

To get a better handle on what marketing automation software is, it's instructive to look at what it isn't. Revenue marketing can only happen when every aspect of your marketing software provides the scalability, predictability, reproducibility, and sustainability with the speed of automation. To take your marketing from expense to asset and to maximize revenue, your marketing tools have to be both powerful and efficient.

Automation is often confused with smaller systems, which is like confusing an inflatable pool with the Atlantic Ocean. Automation is vast and interconnected, carrying huge volumes of trade and making business possible on a global scale; it isn't something you have to inflate yourself. Marketing AI is transformative, not just a larger version of your current marketing process.

More than Email Marketing

Automation makes sending email easier, but that doesn't make *marketing automation* another term for *email marketing*. For automated mailings and retargeting email campaigns, a fully integrated and automated system can pay significant dividends over a system that only manages email. Conventional email marketing has leaned toward impersonal, spray-and-pray techniques in the past, leading readers and Internet service providers (ISPs) to fight back with tighter regulations and antispam software. Marketing automation is a push in the other direction, away from email spam and toward more focused, more finely segmented audiences that are receptive to the messages they receive.

To put it more plainly, marketing automation isn't just a better email tool for you — it's better for your customers.

Email is far from the only task that marketing automation can handle, but it remains one of the most important. Email marketing offers outstanding efficiency, reach, and ROI in a highly measurable format. It's a natural fit for automation and provides a wealth of data that informs other key marketing decisions, from direct mail to telemarketing. Automation ensures that disparate audiences get the right mail at the right time, maximizing open rates and responses.

Automated, But Not Autopiloted

Although marketing automation streamlines marketing flow and provides deeper, more relevant analytics, it is anything but mechanical. With automated systems, companies are better able to understand what their audiences want and delivers it to them. By automating triggered email blasts, creating personal URLs (personal uniform source locators, or

PURLs) for landing pages, and coordinating content with search engine optimization/search engine marketing (SEO/SEM), your marketing team is able to focus on creating outstanding content and enhancing your brand.

Although its analytics and mailing triggers can be set-and-forget events, marketing automation doesn't replace the need for creativity in your content; on the contrary, it's content-rich. With automation, your marketing team has time to develop that customized content. PURLs and JavaScript give every returning visitor a tailor-made landing page uniquely designed to meet that customer's needs. Email, newsletters, and other content offers are also customized to address each marketing segment with highly relevant, targeted information.

Not Just for Big Firms

The first true marketing automation tools belonged solely to the big names. Their extensive IT departments worked on building custom systems for their organizations, while smaller businesses had trouble justifying the expense of such software, even when they had the IT personnel to research and develop it. The new generation of marketing automation software is no longer the province of those few companies. Small, mid- and large-size businesses can all use software-as-a-service (SaaS) marketing automation that puts these powerful tools within the reach of a far broader range of B2B and B2C businesses.

Elements of a MAS

One of the key benefits of marketing automation, particularly for small to midsize firms, is its flexibility. Automation makes you agile, and agility is critical to keeping pace with the ever-changing digital marketplace. Companies can choose which aspects of the software they want to prioritize, redesign the sales and marketing pipeline to optimize flow, and quantify the real value of leads throughout the marketing process. With SaaS, the service provider supplies all the technology and staff necessary at a fraction of the cost of doing it yourself, so that you can focus all of your resources on marketing.

CRM and Marketing Database

Every business needs a customer relationship management (CRM) system, and a complete marketing automation strategy also incorporates these records. The marketing database serves as the system's memory, recording everything about your customers and prospects, including their demographic and firmographic data. With this information, your marketing automation software can develop the well-segmented audiences that enhance the relevance of your marketing message and it lets you customize your content.

Data hygiene and enhancement takes place here to ensure that all your customer records are clean and current. Customers can't respond to messages they never receive, so high deliverability is an important component of any targeted marketing campaign, and a well-organized automated marketing database makes it happen.

Relationship Marketing and the Customer Engagement Engine

As the marketing database is your system's memory, this engine is its nervous system, sending and receiving commands from every part of your integrated marketing campaign while coordinating this information across multiple channels. It's where the potential energy of your leads' information becomes kinetic energy in the form of banner advertising, content marketing, email marketing, retargeting efforts, SEO/SEM, social media, telemarketing, and more. With state-of-the-art automation, your marketing team can get real-time feedback on lead management and progress through the sales funnel.

Behavioral elements can be as predictive as demographics, but in the initial stages of lead generation and lead nurturing, demographic and firmographic data set your baseline. Job function, industry, company size, and other relatively static data form the foundation of your prospects' profiles, but as your marketing automation tools collect behavioral data that reveal how people interact with your brand, you develop a far more sensitive and predictive way to differentiate leads.

Typically, a marketing team lines up the usual suspects when finding target audiences for a campaign. Looking to the usual prospect base by demographics and firmographics alone causes two problems: First, this data provides a snapshot, not a record of actions over time as prospects move through the marketing pipeline. Second, the people you consider your most promising demographic and firmographic leads are just as interesting to your competitors. Firms that look only at this data will find themselves reaching for an increasingly narrow share of a crowded market.

Because firmographic and demographic data is a snapshot, behavioral data is a movie starring your leads. Still images contain plenty of valuable information, but they don't create a narrative the way film can. Behavior based on a lead's activity can be a powerful predictor of the lead's readiness to buy, and automated marketing systems closely track these buying signals.

Analytics

By calibrating, measuring, and optimizing every aspect of your Lead Lifecycle model, your marketing team builds a unified revenue-marketing strategy that transcends activity-focused marketing. Analytics are crucial to the success of your company, because by keeping track of how many leads are moving through each stage of the Lead Lifecycle, your AI can analyze the health of your marketing program and how well your channels, content, and sources are delivering on the promise of sending qualified leads to your sales team. Think of the system's analytics database as its reasoning faculties, delivering feedback about what works and what needs to change. Because the analytics derived from full marketing automation draws from a much deeper knowledge pool, it provides a more nuanced view of your leads, your sales pipeline, and your overall marketing strategy.

Programmers have a saying: "Garbage in, garbage out." In other words, even a sophisticated program can only interpret results based on the original input it receives. Each element of an automated marketing system works in concert and is fully integrated with its counterparts, ensuring more accurate data from the outset. The records in the system's marketing database allow more refined lead segmentation for delivery through the marketing engine, which in turn provides more complete data for lifecycle analysis. It allows you to monitor your funnel weekly or monthly, and to keep track of changes to lead scoring, work-flows, thresholds, lifecycles, and programs. Are qualified leads down? Is the sales team asking for more leads? Is the pace at which the leads move through the funnel increasing or decreasing? Analytics gives you the insight necessary to improve the programs that are having an impact on your revenue. If too few or too many leads are being rejected by sales, your Marketing AI can adjust the lead score. If too many leads are lacking the budget, authority, need, and timing (BANT) required to buy from you, your MAI can improve the quality by tightening the demographics, keywords, and marketing channel qualifications of the sources that you use.

Now that you know what marketing automation is, you need to see how it fits with your current marketing plan. Chapter 2 puts automation in context and gives you a simplified example of how one company's Marketing AI turned a small spend on a webinar into a resounding success.

Takeaways:

1. Marketing AI gives you the ability to scale, reproduce results, predict future revenue, and sustain the growth of your business.
2. Marketing AI is a complete transformation, not just another name for your current marketing processes.
3. Marketing AI increases the speed of leads transiting your sales pipeline by providing the systems and tools necessary to optimize every stage of your Lead Lifecycle model.

CHAPTER 2

Putting Marketing Automation in Context

Henry Ford didn't invent the automobile, but he did something just as important: He pioneered the way to make it better, faster, and less expensive to build than anyone else in a suddenly burgeoning market. Because his factories could turn out identical, well-built Model Ts by the dozen, he almost captured the whole market from the outset.

Today's assembly lines are many generations removed from Ford's. They feature robotic tools and computer controls to keep production moving in a ballet of grace and power, building hundreds of vehicles in the same time it would have taken Ford's team to build a dozen.

Automating simple processes and streamlining production has changed how we make everything, from cars to cakes. The same processes have their virtual counterparts in the marketing sector, making it easier and faster to guide new prospects from entry-level interest to an eventual sale. Marketing automation tools have taken the next step, making it possible to enhance lead generation, as well as nurture leads through your marketing and sales funnel. Because each buyer's journey is different, the way you guide leads along that journey must adapt to meet that prospect's needs.

AI has the potential to revolutionize the marketing industry in the same way that Ford's assembly lines (or later advances in robotics) have, and then some. People aren't cars, and their needs and wants change over time. A Marketing AI is adaptive, allowing you to serve your customers' needs precisely — often even before they've given you their names.

With automation, you go from expense marketing to revenue marketing as you race ahead of your competition. In this chapter you'll learn what marketing automation means for your bottom line and why early adopters are already moving ahead of their competitors.

Marketing Automation in Motion

We often talk about marketing automation in terms of movement, and it's no wonder. Motion is integral to the concept of the sales funnel, and it's one of the biggest reasons to automate. Leads enter at one end of the funnel and progress to an increasing state of sales-readiness until they become buyers. Marketing automation streamlines that process, facilitating your prospects' transformation from new leads to established customers. At the same time, it delivers right-size content with the right amount of detail to stay just a step or two ahead of your prospects on their buyer journeys — far enough ahead to act as a guide but not so far that you lose sight of them.

Before making their ultimate decision to buy, customers first have to become familiar with you, measure your offer against their budget and needs, and move through your sales department's qualifications. At any stage during this journey, many otherwise promising leads drop out of the process. Marketing automation ranks these leads to let your marketing team and sales personnel conserve and convert them.

Your sales department is probably the costliest part of your organization, yet too often marketing fails to qualify leads properly for sales. Divisions between sales and marketing mean the marketing department is essentially tossing leads blindly over a wall and hoping sales personnel are there to catch them. Automation takes down that wall, integrating sales and marketing to ensure that leads are nurtured carefully.

You can also change how widely you open the gate to your lead nurturing process. Establish a connection with only the top scorers in your lead ranking system, and you have a small but highly qualified contact list. Set lower barriers for entry into your marketing campaign, and you build a broader database of prospects to develop and nurture over time.

Automation lets you choose how you market to leads no matter where they're ranked; you can send economical emails to a broader spectrum of leads and save high-ticket approaches for the narrow but highly qualified layer of prospects at the top.

Rhythm and Flow

Every activity your marketing team pursues incurs a cost and produces revenue. Quantifying those costs and revenues using traditional marketing methods is an ongoing challenge, but marketing automation is able to assign values and assess successes on your terms. Because you define what success is, you have an incredibly flexible, fluid system that allows you to direct the flow of leads.

Think of marketing flows as very sophisticated flow charts. Conventional marketing tactics focus on the actions you take, but automation tracks the actions your leads take. Like a true Marketing AI, it can then respond to those actions. When a lead meets the criteria you set for a success, that then-qualified lead receives specific content tailored to his needs. Using state-of-the-art tracking cookies, marketing automation software can build a picture of your leads even before you have their specific data.

Marketing automation lets you control the flow of leads from one end of your marketing pipeline to the other. Triggered actions and reactions keep the drumbeat of your campaigns strong and measured, ensuring that the right lead gets the right message at the right time. Automated systems manage timing for you, delivering introductory messages to new leads and supplying ample information to those in the middle of your sales funnel. As leads reach sales-readiness, they see content that confirms their decision to buy.

Building Your Brand with Marketing AI

You've read how automation controls leads' speed and direction through your sales pipeline, but what about the brand-defining content? What about the captivating creative, the marketing genius who tells your customers who you are and has them lined up to do business with you? Automation is incredibly content-hungry, and content is the heart and soul of brand building. Your Marketing AI excels at delivering content that matters to your audience, but it also gathers the information your marketing team needs to create that relevant content in the first place.

Brand Equity

Building equity in a property means increasing its residual value. Brand equity increases the value of all your marketing efforts by improving visitors' recall, establishing you as an authoritative source and setting you apart from the competition. Branding alone can make the difference in a buying decision. Think that's not true? Consider products like white sugar and aspirin. Everything in your sugar bowl is sucrose, and everything in that bottle you keep in the medicine cabinet is acetylsalicylic acid. They're pure substances, yet manufacturers have spent millions to position themselves as the best brand.

To embrace fully the concept of brand equity, the brand itself has to have intrinsic value. You and your company, not just your products or services, are worth more as a cohesive brand than as a collection of marketing campaigns. Brands have continuity; they persist throughout individual campaigns and across marketing channels. Your buyers take a journey, not a jaunt, and they want a reliable brand to stay with them along the way. That's why branding is critical to B2B industries that have, typically, a longer stretch from initial contact to sale. When so much of what you do relies on reputation, building that reputation through brand equity couldn't be more important.

One of your primary tools for building brand equity is also one of your most accessible: email. You've already read in Chapter 1 about how marketing automation streamlines email creation and mailing; it also offers triggered email options that let you set how, when, and why you mail to your customers. Often your first point of contact with your leads and prospects, email is your initial opportunity to familiarize them with you. Encapsulating your brand in your email ensures that your next communication for future campaigns or retargeting feels familiar, because with email, familiarity breeds sales.

Cross-Channel Branding

What is your company's core identity? What are your values? What role do you play in your customers' daily lives? What problems do you solve? The answers to these questions help define your brand. Successful brand strategies might be built on reliability, innovation, industry knowledge, outstanding service, unique products, or any one of dozens of distinctive values. What you want to emphasize about your brand should take your customers into account, but it's also vital to make it something intrinsic to you, something that doesn't just come from polls and surveys. However you decide to define your brand, expressing it starts with unifying all your marketing across multiple channels into one distinctive voice.

Each channel you use for your marketing has its own strengths. Direct mail lends more legitimacy to your organization and gives customers something tangible to reinforce familiarity. Email is convenient and reaches many people where they spend the most time. Telemarketing is valuable for re-establishing contact with leads that have expressed interest but haven't followed up. SEO helps interested prospects find you on their own. Content marketing informs those prospects and establishes you as an authority. All of these tributaries reinforce your brand but only if they work together.

Here's where marketing automation shines. A single marketer couldn't begin to track a major cross-channel campaign, let alone record and analyze all the data it generates. Automation makes omni-channel marketing so easy that your marketing team can execute in a single day what used to take weeks to orchestrate. You can set up an integrated, three-to-six month campaign in advance and use the software to execute your cross-channel marketing and nurturing campaigns. When omni-channel marketing is this simple, branding falls effortlessly into place.

The Revenue Marketing Revolution

Marketing needs to pay off, and it needs to prove exactly how it's paying off for your company. Automation tracks revenue, as well, showing you precisely where your greatest value is and where you can reallocate your resources for a better return on your investments.

To see how automation empowers revenue marketing, let's take a look at a software company we'll call SEO Schematics, which creates software to monitor search engine rankings and improve optimization. SEO Schematics is a small business that has a limited budget for its latest webinar. The company has a fairly juicy list of leads — 50,000 of them — but the marketing director needs to know how to maximize engagement with these prospects.

With $10,000 to spend, every dollar counts; delivering the maximum return on investment (ROI) is critical to SEO Schematics' future. Data collected from its CRM system and marketing-captured leads via anonymous tracking cookies gives the marketing team cues to its audience's main interests. Those cookies on the company's website, SEO content, and social media channels can later be tied to specific email addresses once leads share their information, so each of the 50,000 marketing-engaged leads in the system get customized, relevant email. The system's automated data hygiene and enhancement features ensure deliverability, so each tailored message finds the right recipient.

Customizing email produces a significant increase in open rates, so instead of the 3 percent open rate the marketing department experienced before automation, a full 6 percent of recipients open their email. These 3,000 email recipients find customized content once they open, and 1,000 of them find those customized calls to action interesting enough to click through to a landing page — or more accurately, to one of a series of customized landing pages the MAS has sent in response to the visitor's browser cookie.

Of the 1,000 leads that click through, many evolve into marketing-qualified leads by exploring the firm's website, following the company on social media, or using a search engine to find more information about the business, all of which marketing automation software can track. Meanwhile, many of these leads' actions trigger additional email communication and build that lead ranking score higher. Over the next few weeks, 20 percent of the original marketing-engaged leads sign up for a webinar and become marketing-qualified leads. Out of those 200 webinar sign-ups, 100 become attendees and move on to become sales-accepted and sales-qualified leads.

If the initial outlay for the webinar campaign was $10,000 and resulted in 100 leads, then the company's real cost per sales–qualified lead is $100. If the average customer's transaction is $5,000, and if a group of sales-qualified leads has a 30 percent conversion rate, this marketing campaign was a huge success. Quantifying that success every step of the way with marketing automation ensures a better ROI on future campaigns, and builds a more complete data picture which points out the most effective flow paths through the sales pipeline.

We discussed SPRS in Chapter 1. Here's how its elements contributed to an effective campaign for SEO Schematics in the short term, and to its successful revenue marketing strategy in the long term:

- ➤ **Scalability:** The initial mailing was to 50,000 leads, but as the company grows the software can scale to an unlimited number of leads and return the same 6 percent open rate. Automated marketing allows businesses to extrapolate and interpolate expected revenue anywhere along a sliding scale. For sales departments defining their quotas or finance departments developing next year's budget, scalability is key.

- ➤ **Predictability:** By being able to predict how many leads would open, click through, sign up, attend, and eventually convert, the automated system informed the marketing team's decisions about the number of initial emails sent and about any subsequent contact with leads.

- ➤ **Reproducibility:** Controlling and optimizing the pace at which leads are nurtured and moved through the sales funnel for one campaign is important; being able to perform the same magic again and again is the foundation for lasting success.

- ➤ **Sustainability:** SEO Schematics is able not only to enjoy success with this campaign, but it can also use the process as a learning experience for the Marketing AI. Armed with new knowledge, the MAI can now respond intelligently to future events. As the marketplace changes, as it inevitably will, the Marketing AI will keep pace for sustained success.

In an actual campaign, options are more varied and nuanced, addressing a far wider range of possibilities and contingencies. In fact, any campaign would quickly become too complex to manage by hand. Automation isn't just a luxury here; it's a necessity for revenue marketing.

Summing It Up: A Dozen Benefits of Marketing AI

We'll go into more detail later about how automation affects every aspect of marketing, but here's a rundown of the most salient points:

1. Turn the setup for multitouch campaigns into one-day events: Email marketing, direct mail, website landing pages, social media, content marketing, and SEO are all critical for connecting with your prospects. Coordinating them, gathering results, and analyzing that information without automation would take a team weeks to complete.

2. Establish automated actions that respond to behaviors: When leads open an email, click a link, or download content from your site, their actions automatically trigger a cascade of events that flow naturally from your customers' choices.

3. Assign and notify sales team when a lead is generated: Nothing increases the likelihood of converting prospects to customers better than responding quickly to leads when they're ready for a sales associate to call. No other software system integrates sales and marketing as part of the same seamless pipeline the way marketing automation can.

4. Produce custom scoring that transitions each lead through the Lead Lifecycle to identify purchase readiness: By assigning a score to every action your lead takes, you identify when the prospect is ready for a sales call while prospects who aren't quite ready move through a customized lead nurturing process. At every step of lead nurturing, the software tracks lead quality, sales readiness, and the speed and progression of lead conversion through the sales funnel. You'll learn more about how to

use key performance indicators (KPIs) and lead scoring strategies in Chapter 5.

5. Personalize and connect content through all channels: No two prospects are the same. They react to content and campaigns differently. Marketing automation tracks which channels, content, and efforts prospects respond to best so that you can target them with the most effective campaigns.

6. Manage different types of marketing efforts from one central location: Think of marketing automation software as a captain's bridge, the nexus from which you and your marketing team manage everything. Content marketing, email, retargeting campaigns, customer loyalty programs, lead generation, lead scoring, gathering and enhancing data, advertising — your team can coordinate every aspect of your marketing campaigns with one integrated system.

7. Define the assets and flow actions of your campaigns with one platform: Every change in your campaign can have a profound effect on every other element. That's why a complete marketing automation toolset is absolutely essential to the mastery of omnichannel campaigns.

8. Create and manage emails, forms, landing pages, and SEO within a single platform: Unifying your marketing materials creates a seamless experience for customers and makes managing new campaigns simple. Your marketing automation specialist can clone, alter, and reshape campaign elements with a few clicks, making it easy to repeat and improve on your successes.

9. Use real-time creative optimization: Make your website and your email campaigns more relevant and responsive by displaying content that most interests your lead based on the products, services, emails, and web pages that they've visited and responded to.

10. Dynamically personalize content within email and online based on audiences' unique behaviors and demographics: Connect with your audiences more fully when you show them personalized content tailor-made for their needs.

11. Follow audience's lineage from email delivery to its web activity: Knowing what prompted a client to visit your site, click through on your email, or make a purchase is critical to improving the customer's experience and success of your lead-generation programs. Automation tools give you an in-depth view into your marketing pipeline.

12. Trigger an automated response for every action or inactivity demonstrated by your audience: With today's marketing technology, prospects and customers gauge the reputation of your company based on how quickly you respond to their requests. The most successful companies use software-enabled, automatically triggered actions that interpret the request and respond with lightning speed.

In Part II you'll learn the basics of data integrity and hygiene. Without a data governance strategy, your data will send conflicting, confusing signals, and your marketing programs will never achieve the high level of ROI and performance your company deserves. Working with clean, centralized data is the first step to a successful marketing campaign cycle, and in Chapter 3 you'll find out how automation makes that happen. Chapter 4 illustrates how profiling, cloning, and append services fill in the blanks about your leads so that you can deliver customized, relevant content to an audience you thoroughly understand.

Takeaways:

1. Automation makes omni-channel marketing so easy that what used to take weeks can be executed in a single day.

2. Automation simplifies your marketing and streamlines production with enhanced lead generation and lead nurturing processes that deliver relevant content at each stage of the buyer's journey.

3. Delivering relevant content that matters to your audience keeps the prospect moving forward in the sales funnel.

Part II

Discovery: Building Your Central Intelligence

CHAPTER 3

CENTRAL INTELLIGENCE AND DATA GOVERNANCE

Apainter needs a clean canvas. A chef needs a well-organized kitchen. Your creative team needs to work in a clean, well-organized space, and that comes from strong data governance. Identifying inactive or inaccurate records and purging them from the database is critical to effective marketing. To put it more plainly, you're wasting time and money if you're trying to send a message to someone who no longer lives at that address or works at that company.

Your goal with data governance is complete data — not complex data. It's easy to get trapped within the complexity of your data, especially when records are isolated. Today's executives are being held to a higher degree of accountability that can only come from proper data governance. It's no longer acceptable to measure results by the number of clicks or business cards collected. Quantity is no substitute for quality. Analog methods used in the past have given way to a new breed of executives who are laser focused on profitable, quantifiable returns.

To manage the information you gain and make that knowledge actionable, it needs to be in one place. Over the past several years, the business world has experienced a revolutionary shift in the role marketing plays in an organization's success. Take a good look at any business that has rocketed to the Fortune 500, and you'll find a company dependent on three key factors: the centralization, normalization, and optimization of data — a process we call central intelligence alignment (CIA).

Central Intelligence

Think back to the last time you bought a new computer or smartphone. You probably weren't able to transfer all your information seamlessly, and had to enter some of it by hand. Now take the complexity of managing that individual amount of data and extrapolate to billions of data points across multiple sales channels and millions of leads. How do you centralize information and make it useful for marketing and sales? How do you make that data actionable? A well-executed CIA strategy supplies your Marketing AI with what it needs to be fully functional.

Using the CIA method means pulling all your separate silos of information together (centralizing them). Normalization then standardizes that information. Last, optimization focuses the business intelligence to create actionable insights, to allow seamless automation, and to transform businesses into innovators. Amazon, Facebook, Google, Nest, Netflix, Pandora, and Uber have all used this CIA strategy to vanquish their brick-and-mortar counterparts.

Marketing has become the hub where finance, technology, information, and analytics intersect to build powerful new competitors. The CIO strategy underlies the highest level of growth and performance, revenue marketing. Revenue performance marketing replaces uncertainty with a model that confidently predicts a company's future ROI that is scalable, repeatable, and sustainable.

Centralization

To have a fully functional artificial intelligence, you must start by centralizing that intelligence. It's the nerve center that receives all the messages your leads are sending you about what they need to become a customer. When you're able to process all these seemingly unrelated bits of information into a coherent whole, you have the key that unlocks rapid growth for your business.

You can't have islands of knowledge and expect to have a functional AI. Like a person with amnesia, the system won't be able to link essential facts. It may contain plenty of data, but it no longer works as a useful artificial intelligence. Unless it has all the necessary data in one place and a set of rules with which to handle that information, your AI is unable to draw inferences about what your prospects need or whether they are a good match for what you offer. To identify the genuine opportunities and eliminate wasted resources, your system must be based on centralized data.

Every time you ask your leads to take action, you inevitably create buying friction, an innate resistance to moving forward. With centralization, your Marketing AI is aware of all the knowledge leads have already given you, so you don't ask for it again. Centralizing data reduces impediments to action. As you pool all your resources, you know more about your prospects and are able to track their forward momentum through the Lead Lifecycle (Prologue and Chapter 5).

Centralizing your data — bringing everything about your leads (your accounting system, email marketing database, in-house list of direct mail addresses, social, pay-per-click (PPC), and CRM files) together — gives your Marketing AI what it needs to make complex data simple and usable. Centralization is the foundation of everything else we discuss in *Marketing AI: From Automation to Revenue Performance Marketing,* because it's fundamental to your AI's learning and interpretation. But it's only part of the puzzle.

Normalization

Take a look at your company's common drive. Unless you've created a centralized rule set for data storage, you probably see a hodgepodge of naming conventions. When left to their own devices, people differ dramatically in their organizational methods. Others can usually piece together what these different systems mean, but your Marketing AI isn't a person. It doesn't immediately recognize different formats and needs information that's put into a cohesive, standardized form — in other words, data that's normalized.

Intelligent systems are far more literal than people. They use a rulebook (a sort of data dictionary) to guide and process information. A lead can fill out a form as "Bill Larson" from "IBM" one time and "William Larson" from "International Business Machines" on the next visit. Without algorithms to recognize and group these variant data elements together into a single account, a computer will treat Bill and William as two different people. When your marketing system understands that they are the same person, it can follow all that individual's actions as he interacts with you so you won't miss the buying signals when this lead is ready to buy.

Inconsistency is the death knell for databases, making them all but unusable. Normalization creates consistency throughout your database. By creating a standardized framework making data recognizable, all the information it contains is instantly accessible and actionable, to your literal-minded AI.

A Marketing AI using its data dictionary to normalize the information properly translates the similarities in each form and cross-references to see that they all belong in the same group. By seeing that all these forms are linked to the same company name, IP address, activity, and other details, the MAI forms a clear portrait of this potential customer and correctly attributes all his demographic profiles and signals of interest to a single person.

Optimization

When your data's centralized and normalized, it's also possible to compare it as a whole or in segments against an existing database. It opens new markets to you, lets you maximize the value of your lists, and allows you to append data that connects all your information from disparate sources into a cohesive whole.

Data optimization is fundamental to data-driven revenue-performance marketing. It is the process by which you optimize your Lead Lifecycle. Standardizing and optimizing your data allows your Marketing AI to score leads as they progress through the sales funnel and accurately gauges their interest. Instead of looking at individual records, the system is able to aggregate information in meaningful ways and to understand relationships between data points.

Let's look at a company that markets almost exclusively to small businesses. More than 80 percent of its revenue comes from small businesses, so pinpointing this audience segment is vital to the company's revenue-performance marketing strategy. It was difficult to do that with the company's old database. The original database had thousands of records with the actual employee size (e.g., 24 or 121) attached to them. The company created a set of standardization ranges that aggregated this data into five meaningful segments: "Fewer than 49 employees," "50-100 employees," "100-499 employees," "500-999 employees," and "1,000 or more employees."

Working with these normalized segments, the new system is able to optimize the database. When evaluating five elements instead of thousands, it only takes a glance to see where the company should and shouldn't concentrate its marketing efforts. It simplifies the process that applies a higher lead score to records in the segments with the lower employee sizes.

The Cost of Bad Data

Who's in charge of your CIA? Who gets your CRM and your marketing automation system to synchronize with ease? Who defines your data dictionary?

Let's explore how bloated data costs you in real terms. One cost is direct; most CRM costs are defined on a per-name basis, and a database full of invalid names is like a property with vacant spaces to fill. If you're the property owner, each of those unused spaces costs you money while returning no revenue. You can automate your data governance and synchronize your data using an automated API process based on time, events, data age, and data content. Automated data governance acts as a sort of property manager, ensuring that each of these spaces is filled where possible, and eliminated when necessary. By defining match codes, pieces of data that are used to index information, and conducting merge/purge operations with these fixed indices in place, a data governance strategy ensures that the only information your Marketing AI eliminates is the unwanted kind — duplicate names, invalid addresses and other data bloat. Cleaner data from the outset and populates your list with high-quality leads.

Data doesn't exist in a vacuum. It's contextual, especially if it's behavioral data. That's why a MAS installation is not the same as implementation, and why even automated processes need a data governance manager (DGM) to set the rules of the universe in which your Marketing

AI does its work. When properly set up and maintained, your MAS is an active participant in automated data hygiene and enhancement, not just a tool. A Marketing AI helps you and your DGM identify duplicate records, reduce bloat, and spot opportunities when the data landscape changes, as it inevitably will.

Set Your Data Hygiene Rules

Before you touch your current database, you need to define your standards for list hygiene. Your Marketing AI is a system that relies on reinforcement learning to understand its environment, so defining that environment accurately with a complete, well-constructed data dictionary is critical. Consider the following questions and use them to show your MAS which data matters most:

1. What is your database's current state of health? Has it been cleaned regularly throughout its existence, or is it long overdue for a thorough scrubbing?

2. What are your minimum standards for deliverability? You may find, as many business owners do, that your records follow the 80/20 rule — that is, the 20 percent of your customers with the most complete records account for 80 percent of your sales.

3. How complete must records be to stay in the database? Fragmentary records don't give your Marketing AI enough information to make decisions about how to nurture these leads. By cross-referencing records and filling in the blanks with data appends, your automation system is able to respond to what your customers need, giving them the right information at the right time.

4. Where are your break points for information recency and activity? In some industries, orders are large and infrequent. Others rely on frequent but smaller sales. Your answer to this question determines when your marketing automation system moves older records to a different nurturing flow or archives them altogether.

5. What information should you request? Email addresses that can be used in a nurture campaign or serve as match codes are

of high importance, while phone numbers and social handles might be lower on your priority list.

6. How do you acquire your data? When using a MAS, you're already compiling some information on your customers via browser cookies long before they become customers. But setting constraints on the information you get from your contacts can result in more sales-qualified leads. For example, prepopulated forms are a nice convenience for visitors, but they introduce errors and outdated information into a database. It's better to require input of some fields or have a set schedule for erasing prepopulated information so users re-enter current data. This new information then gets normalized and linked with the appropriate lead's account.

7. Which data should you use? Some prospects use multiple information sets, and your MAI needs to use the data your customers prefer. It's a good practice to create more than one field for email address, for example. The first field contains the original email address that was initially provided by the contact. The other, a field labeled "preferred email address," contains the most recent email address provided. Your Marketing AI can then match the two fields to confirm if it is a new email address or a duplicate according to your CIA rules.

Keep in mind that your marketing team can redefine the environment for the system, so it's flexible. If you find you haven't sufficiently pared records for frequency and recency to result in cleaner data, for example, you can adjust these parameters. We'll get into the analytics that tell you which way you should adjust your data-hygiene rules for maximum effect in Chapter 18, but for now it's important just to remember that you and your DGM control the dials here.

Cleanse Your Database

For most companies lead generation is the costliest aspect of their marketing department's activity. According to a Marketing Sherpa survey, more than 64 percent of responding companies said they invested greater than $20 per lead, and more than one in three invested over $100 per lead. Those are startling figures, but they become even more shocking when you realize that the greatest impact of inaccurate or inactive data is on lead generation. Few companies can afford to throw those efforts away, and fewer still can afford to miss out on a host of potentially profitable leads because of an ISP blacklist.

Discovery depends on clean data, and clean data should have regular check-ups. With marketing automation, you're able to set regular times and triggers for updates and health checks. All data has a natural decay rate, but frequent contact-data checks and automated updates offset that decay and preserve important information. Database hygiene and management tools now track people's movements to new homes or jobs, merge information when it's inadvertently duplicated, and identify records that need attention. The message is clear: Clean data costs less and delivers more.

If you had to hunt down and remove inaccurate and inactive data on your own, you'd spend years on even a small customer list. Thanks to automation, the process now takes an afternoon or so. Like most maintenance tasks, database cleaning has a multipoint inspection system that ensures cleanliness. Following are seven key elements that marketing automation experts examine when assessing a database's health and keeping it clean.

1. **Deliverability** – Ideally, all your mail, email, and phone correspondence would reach the person you wanted to find every time you reached out to your customer. In the real world that's rarely possible, and larger databases inevitably have a few undeliverable results. You and your marketing team can determine what your expected deliverable rate is, but 90 percent for direct mail and 95 percent for email is a good starting point. If you see deliverability rates lower than these, your database is overdue for pruning.

2. **Lead Generation** – Are messages designed for lead generation increasing or decreasing in effectiveness? A decline in lead-generation rates could indicate lax database hygiene. (This could also be an indicator of poor marketing segmentation — a concept we'll discuss in Chapter 4 — or a problem with lead scoring, which you'll learn about in Chapter 5.)

3. **Reputable Partners** – If you've built your own list, you know how much time and effort goes into it. One way to instantly increase your marketing reach is through reputable list-brokerage companies. Choose companies that have a proven record of good data husbandry for your list rental. Using reliable sources that practice excellent list hygiene results in valuable new leads without concerns about low delivery rates and hits to your reputation.

4. **Hard and Soft Bounce Records** – A hard bounce means email is permanently undeliverable. It usually means the email address doesn't exist or has been closed. Typically, names that result in a hard bounce immediately come off the list. Soft bounces are more complex; they mean the email wasn't deliverable at this time but may make it through on a subsequent attempt. A soft bounce can happen for a number of reasons: Temporary loss of service on the user's side or a full mailbox are two possibilities. But they also need to be watched closely. Best practices dictate that three or more consecutive soft bounces should result in removing the address from the active database.

5. **Sender Scores** – ISPs have a keen interest in protecting their users' in-boxes, so maintaining a high sender score is paramount. Fewer hard and soft bounces from undeliverable or blocked addresses raise your sender score. Higher sender scores mean a better reputation among ISPs, and a sterling reputation is your invitation to your prospects' email as a trusted source. Your Marketing AI monitors your daily sender score for you, tracking key performance indicators such as delivery rates and inbox penetration.

6. **Duplicate Data** – Duplicate information is sometimes introduced into databases. It can happen when improperly synching with your CRM or when whole lists merge. Other times, duplicates come from users who forget a password or sign up under a different email address. Merging and purging processes keep incremental information and remove the duplicates, keeping your list compact and compliant with your data-governance rules.

7. **Updates** – When a customer moves or forwards mail to another address, updating that information is vital to getting messages

where they need to go. Updating records is also vital for effective data appending services, a key aspect of data enhancement.

8. **Recency** – Older information that has had no activity can go in a couple of different directions. With some of your best customers, you may want to roll records into a slow-drip retargeting campaign. With others, you will want to warehouse information. Over time some of these records can become active again, but even if they don't, that data's useful for research. No data is ever wasted. You will also breathe fresh life into these leads by using a data-append service to validate the current postal and email address or append a new one.

Data Enhancement — Append and Reverse Append

Serving relevant content is key to successful marketing. Information that lets you identify common traits between your prospects and your best customers is hard to identify without the data that forms a complete picture. Relevance is king, but how do you establish it? That's the purpose of the discovery process, and one of the most powerful tools at your disposal is data appending. A specific form of data optimization, appending matches the information you already have with information on a third-party database to build a more complete view of an individual customer. Appending matches company name and postal addresses to active emails; reverse appending uses email addresses to append street address, phone number, and firmographic information.

In most cases email is the most cost-effective solution for connecting with your prospects. Physical mailing addresses also contain a tremendous amount of valuable data. Appends bring these key elements together to enhance the power of each. Customers who once only connected with you in one area now receive impressions via additional marketing avenues — a key tenet of omni-channel-marketing strategies. Every bit of data you discover through appends not only improves your chances of connecting with your buyers, it also gives your marketing automation system another means to cross-reference and fill in additional blanks.

Reliable, consistent data gives you reliable, consistent results. By profiling your data against an existing database and against other files within the system itself, you're able to weed out invalid data and leave only relevant information. Inefficient or undersized append services can't cross-reference data the way a larger, more powerful system can. You need a large pool of data — think tens of millions of names, not tens of thousands — to get the most out of appending, but it has the power to teach your Marketing AI a wealth of new information.

Tracking People in Motion

Conventional data collection works solely to amass information and makes only a rudimentary attempt at analysis. It doesn't track people as they move through a marketing and sales pipeline or open a window on how they interact with your brand over time.

Let's look at our test case once again. As SEO Schematics' executives make the move from siloed marketing systems to a complete Marketing AI using the CIA process, they gain a new perspective by bringing time and motion into their analytics. Instead of seeing how many people visited their website and looking at which pages these prospects visited, the system now reveals how long visitors stayed on a page and tracks where they traveled next. It records subsequent visits over time via anonymous browser cookies, building a picture of a potential customer's needs even before that visitor has shared her name.

If you know how your prospects become buyers, the turning points they reach, the pathways they take in your sales pipeline, and what they need to advance through it, you'll unlock the secrets of scaling up your organization's profits. Your Marketing AI is the key to understanding how your customers interact with your brand and contextualizing their behavior.

As adults we learn how to place information in context and build a more nuanced concept of our universe. By understanding the simplest rules and contextualizing them, we're able to derive more complex information from our environments as we learn and put that complexity into a simple framework for easy access.

Your marketing automation system discovers and learns, too, but because the knowledge it needs is highly specialized and the data it uses to gain that knowledge comes in at lightning-fast speeds, it goes through the process far more quickly than any human mind could manage.

Each sale represents the final decision in a long chain of choices your customer had to make. Long before making that buying decision, customers first had to become aware that they need the products and services you offer, become familiar with you, measure your offer against those offered by your competitors, decide if it meets their budget and needs, and move through your sales department's qualifications. At any stage during this journey, many otherwise promising leads drop out of the process. Marketing automation ranks these leads to let your marketing and sales team conserve and convert them. But to rank leads, the system must first understand which buying signals your customers are sending. That's where discovery through firmographic, demographic, behavioral, and contextual data comes in.

Once it discovers that your best customers have certain traits in common or that a certain behavior's strongly correlated with sales readiness, it remembers these basics, giving you the chance to build on them. This kind of responsive learning is the foundation of Marketing AI, and it's what differentiates this responsive, sensitive system from a set of simple tools designed to record information without analysis.

In Chapter 4 you'll follow your MAS as it pieces these individual data points of names, email addresses, buying habits, and site traffic histories into buyer profiles that show you a broader view of your customers and where you'll find more of them. You'll learn about your customers' buying DNA and discover why customer profiles are essential to your company's future health and success.

Takeaways:

1. Central Intelligence — the centralization, normalization, and optimization of data — is the essential component of successful marketing automation.
2. Automate and synchronize your data using a computerized API process constructed on a set of data governance rules based on time, events, data age, and data content.
3. Using the CIA process, you'll build a solid picture of a potential customer's needs even before that visitor has shared their name.

CHAPTER 4

CUSTOMER PROFILES AND CLONING

Chapter 3 introduced you to the building blocks of the discovery process, the first steps your Marketing AI takes as it learns to walk, then run — then soar. Here, you'll understand how that raw data comes together to form the architecture of your marketing plan by building highly detailed customer profiles and cloning. Customer portraits aren't a new concept to marketers, but automation takes these images from two-dimensional snapshots to full-length feature films about your buyers. Once you have that film in place, you can use it to find and catalog other films in the same or similar genres, building a library of masterworks.

Who Are Your Customers?

Marketing today is about relevant, compelling, engaging content and inviting your prospects to learn more about you, none of which is possible if you don't know as much as possible about your customers and why they became your customers. Before we get into how to create successful, high-yield campaigns consistently, we'll show you how to identify who your customers and prospects are so you can define the content and pathways needed to guide them through your marketing pipeline.

To develop customer profiles, you and your marketing automation team leverage your current buyer retention data to develop a sound customer acquisition strategy. The positive effects on customer retention are readily apparent when you speak the language your buyers most want to hear. Because profiling and understanding your customer plays such a pivotal role in the cloning process, it also has a dramatic impact on customer acquisition. Following is a deeper look at those two concepts and how they work together.

Customer Acquisition and Retention

When you're speaking to a new prospect, you're talking to someone who has more to learn about you before making a buying decision. Figuring out how long it takes to make that decision is a complex process for you *and* your prospect, but your MAI is uniquely equipped to help determine that and to speed decision-making.

You know that about 50 percent of a buyer's journey takes place before your prospect ever comes in contact with your sales staff — people do their research long before they buy. You still have something to prove to them; if you do it well, you have a winning customer acquisition strategy. Your prospects have done their homework on you and with effective profiling; you are also armed with knowledge. Cloning helps you understand a few vital details about your prospects before you make contact. You already have your existing customers' DNA, so you can find prospects whose marketing footprint matches most closely with that of the people who already buy from you.

Customer retention must also be a high priority for any successful revenue-marketing plan. The DNA of your existing customer base extends far beyond demographics and behavioral scores. Developing a deep, thorough understanding of how your customers interact with you by assessing their specific interest in the products and services you offer closely correlates with sales now and into the future.

Firmographic information, such as job function, industry, and company size, can be very predictive of purchasing affinities. Contextual data, including groupings by product, topical interests, and web-page taxonomies, also can be used to determine cross- and upsell, and other retention strategies that are crucial to growing your business. This data can also help influence future customers' behavior by using contextual information to match customer buying histories and content campaigns streamed to new, qualified leads. Customers who like what you offer are predisposed to be loyal, but as in any relationship, you need to put in some effort too. Your MAS helps you decipher what your customers want and how to give them more of it, which is the heart of customer retention. You can't be relevant until you know your customers' needs. Meet those needs and explain how you'll continue to meet them, and you'll turn loyal customers into referral sources and referral sources into advocates for your business.

The intersection of retention and acquisition is difficult for many marketers to navigate. Making the leap from data you already know to information you can use to grow is a significant challenge without automation to streamline the discovery process. The sooner you move outside your comfort zone and use predictive data, customer profiles, and cloning to enhance your acquisition prospecting, the greater your potential growth can be. It's easy to rest on past successes and continue to reap profits from your current customers, but even the most loyal customer base suffers attrition.

It isn't enough to meet that replacement rate; you need to exceed it to grow. With buyer personas and cloning, you're able not only to top your customer replacement rate, but also potentially double or triple it. This is big change, and to handle it, you need MAS that can handle big data.

Big Data for Building Customer Profiles

What artists do with paint and editors do with film, marketing automation software does with information, using a collection of individual data points to put together a vivid picture of your customer base. With it, you can develop customer personas to inform your marketing decisions, understand the broader trends underlying your clients' behavior, and streamline the flow of prospects through your sales and marketing pipeline.

Sometimes it's hard to spot evolving trends from the surface, but with marketing AI you get a top-down perspective that lets you identify a shift as it begins. Marketing automation goes many steps beyond conventional marketing tools, not only analyzing data as a whole and creating composite customer personas, but also highlighting changes in real-time. It adds a behavioral component to discovery, allowing you to see how your prospects interact with your brand and giving you an understanding of the environment that's conducive to closing sales.

Marketing automation systems embed anonymous browser cookies and JavaScript to find out more about your leads: How did they find your page, how long did they stay on it, and what did they click while on your site? Understanding how people interact with your site, collecting anonymous data about their behavior, and building customer personas based on composite data, gives you a clear picture of how promising leads connect with you.

By making that connection between certain customer behaviors and sales readiness right away, placing them in an understandable, easily accessible context, your MAI shines a spotlight on the your content and analyzes what works best, precisely what makes it such an effective conversion tool. Using that data to predict how future visitors will convert to customers tells you where your leads are and how best to reach them.

When you watch a movie, you aren't seeing movement; you're seeing individual still frames. Your brain is where the real magic happens, smoothing and connecting a series of static images into a dazzling action sequence, an exciting chase scene, or an impassioned kiss. Your marketing message becomes a finely produced movie when your potential customers see a seamlessly integrated marketing message that gives them the information they need to make buying decisions precisely when they want it.

Big Data: The Four Vs

Modern marketers amass incredible amounts of data — more data than any single person or team of marketers could analyze to construct profiles — to construct customer profiles prior to cloning. Assembling a coherent customer profile from information spread across multiple platforms takes huge computing power, and it's changing how modern marketing looks. To get a better understanding of the science behind buyer personas and to see how they relate to your marketing strategy, let's look at how data scientists define big data.

Volume

It may sound redundant, but big data is really big. It's so big, in fact, that people can't readily imagine or manipulate it without an automated system to process the information. And big data isn't a few thousand customer names, or even a few hundred thousand. Only when you move into the realm of millions and billions of data points do you start to see big data analysis truly shine. That doesn't mean you need millions of customers to see big data applications in action; you just need a few customers whose collective behavioral, firmographic, demographic, and contextual information adds up to millions of interrelated data points.

Velocity

Not only must your system chew through mountains of data, it has to do it quickly. Data streams through the system at speeds far too fast to follow, giving your marketing program far greater flexibility. One of the biggest issues with conventional systems is their immobility. Customer personas can and do change over time, so a static system that doesn't learn from and respond to its environment lacks the speed to change with your audience.

Variety

Data comes from many sources, and big data can assemble and analyze them all. That's especially necessary in marketing as cross-channel data has historically been difficult to compare. How do you know if your blog resonates with each segment of your audience? How do you match website downloads with email opens and describe the relationship between these actions in terms of sales readiness? How do you create a buyer profile that includes multiple layers of data, and how do you assign this profile to the correct audience segment? A marketing automation system will tell you how because it can handle the tremendous variety that's the hallmark of modern digital marketing.

Veracity

We discussed it in Chapter 3 and we're stressing it again here: Your data has to be clean to be accurate. When your data's uncertain, your results are uncertain, too. Without certainty and consistency, companies aren't able to generate predictive buyer models that tell them where their next customers may be found. A MAS maintains clean records across multiple channels, cross-referencing and appending vital information when possible to generate more accurate, complete records.

B2B Profiles in Three Levels

The principles of Marketing AI work equally well for B2C and B2B applications, but B2B marketing involves additional layers of data that inform every step of your marketing process. If your customers are business professionals, there are identifiers critical to producing an effective profile that sheds light on your current clients, while helping you generate the information needed to acquire more like them. Business profiles break into three fundamental levels: site, individual, and contact.

On the contact level, you must have complete, clean data about each customer, so the goal is to collect or append all contact points. This is the most fundamental level of information about the people you're reaching, including first names, last names, company names, postal addresses, phone numbers, and email addresses. These are the building blocks we talked about in Chapter 3, or the single frames that make up the epic film that is each buyer's journey.

Everyone who works for a company also has another layer of information that describes that person's role within it. On this individual level, you want to know your customers' job titles, responsibilities, and purchasing authority. You're speaking to the position, rather than to the person who is your contact, so this data set may remain consistent as personnel change within your target businesses. Your marketing message has far greater impact when it reaches people in a position to act on it directly, so collecting and appending data at the individual level is vital. Think of this level as sets within that metaphorical movie, sets that different actors may move through but that remain consistent throughout the film.

At the site level you want to know firmographic data about the company, including number of employees (are you speaking to small companies or Fortune 1,000 firms?), sales volume (as more technology firms emerge, sales volume can be a telling metric), standard industrial classification (SIC), which defines the type of business or industry your sales lead is in (a key piece of data that's the foundation of sales strategy and personalization to your prospects and customers), and site penetration. Site penetration is a vital statistic that tells you how many contacts you have at a company, which of them are potential customers, and whether you can benefit from expanding your reach within it.

Note that demographic and firmographic information at every level appears relatively static compared with the constant shifts in behavioral data, which applies to all three levels. If trying to visualize many levels of granularity for three separate types of data, all of which change at different speeds, is making you feel a little like you're trying to watch three movies at once, you're starting to see why a Marketing AI is essential to 21st-century marketing. Automation coordinates pieces of information that are difficult to visualize effortlessly, and unites them into a cohesive whole.

Building a Total Customer Profile for Cloning

If you could condense your entire customer base to 10 representative customers, you would undoubtedly spot some interesting similarities and trends that are difficult to see when looking at thousands or millions of real individuals. You might notice that four or five of your representative customers have a large overlap in interests while others might not have as much in common. A Marketing AI can see that big picture comprising millions, and translate it into a handful of customer personas via profiling. Profiling for marketers means creating an accurate portrait of your customers so you know how to be relevant to other prospects that have a lot in common with them. With profiling, you're able to recognize those areas of common ground; with cloning, you find others who share the same territory.

Let's look at your 10 representative customers again. You could learn a lot about them if you could hear their conversations and know more about how they relate to one another. That's the kind of insight a MAS delivers. If you were to invite another two or three customers to your party, would you know where to send the invitations and who might be most interested in receiving them? Your Marketing AI can give you some idea, but otherwise, it's hard to guess where your next great market might be.

Before you answer, think about what you want to accomplish by inviting more guests. Every business can say it wants to expand its customer base and increase profits, but it isn't enough to know generalities. Specificity leads to relevance, and relevance leads directly to better customer retention and acquisition.

Once you've defined those 10 people at your party, you can clone them to attract new customers. A cloned prospect contains characteristics that are similar to those your customers already have. This is one of the more challenging aspects of marketing, but it's also richly rewarding. Helping a business thrive by expanding its reach instead of staying within its safe zone is gratifying for marketers, but the real benefits go to the businesses themselves. It's as important to maximize the revenue you are generating from your existing retention customers as it is to generate dollar one from a prospect that becomes a new customer or acquisition, and a sound profiling process achieves both.

Finding and Cloning Your Best Customers

All 10 customers at your gathering are important, but some are truly the life of the party. Some of them bring guests — that is, new prospects — in the form of referrals and highly visible brand loyalty. Others are big spenders and bring lavish gifts for the host. By locating those party guests and inviting more just like them, you reap tremendous benefits. It's the 80/20 rule in action again: 20 percent of your customers probably account for 80 percent of your business. Think of them as that fascinating couple you always want to invite to your next gala event.

As with all profiles, the first step to finding ideal customer profiles (ICPs) and cloning their DNA is working with the cleanest data possible. Without a clean database, you're relying on potentially inaccurate information that could throw off your results by orders of magnitude, especially since your sample set is now smaller than profiling your entire customer base. Merging and purging data, segmenting by recency, and enhancing data with append services maximize your accuracy when filling in the blanks on your ideal customer base.

Useful customer profiles depend on what you want those customers to do, and that's why your Marketing AI analyzes your results, creates audience segments, and frames certain defining characteristics as key performance indicators for those segments. Depending on your campaign and where you'd most like to grow, you might look at the people who have the highest overall sales, the highest per-sale volume or the greatest purchase frequency. If your industry is highly seasonal, for example, you could realize the greatest gains from looking at frequent buyers and cloning them to court others who will supply you with a more stable off-season income. Other common customer KPIs include:

- **Customer loyalty** – Who has been with you longest, and why are they the standard-bearers for loyalty? This metric is especially valuable for businesses with a high churn rate in their customer base.

- **Recency** – Have you experienced a boom in one market segment within the past quarter or two? Such growth spikes are rich opportunities for spotting a nascent market niche and filling it before competitors even know it's there.

- **Engagement** – You know some people in your intended audience are paying closer attention. They are regularly opening your emails, downloading your content and attending your webinars. Finding them and looking for more like them will increase your open and click rates, which in turn leads to a wider and more responsive customer base. Keep this metric in mind when you're ready to expand initial contact lists.

- **Gold-star customers** – These are the customers who reach for the gourmet coffee, spring for first-class plane tickets, and invest in your premium services. Look to these highly involved customers who are willing to spend a little extra to get upgraded products and services to see how you can attract more of them with cloned profiles.

- **Referral magnets** – Some customers may not be your most lavish spenders or your longest-lived loyalists, but they have great connections and deserve to be valued highly too. Referrers are advocates for your business and are an excellent way of generating high-quality leads, so create a profile of your frequent referrers to find more of them and encourage others to follow in their footsteps.

Cloning in the Wild

We'll say it again: You can't be relevant if you don't know who your customer is. Marketing to third-party lists and online communities using top 20 percent cloned customer profiles instantly gives you some knowledge of your audience so you aren't starting cold.

With clean, complete data that has been thoroughly evaluated and prioritized, you're ready to take your buyer personas and clone them outside your current customer base. Databases containing tens of millions of members work with cloned profiles to generate lists of customers who closely match those characteristics and typically behave in the same manner as their associates in the same marketing segment.

No amount of guesswork can compare to a thorough discovery process through data hygiene, enhancement, and evaluation into usable ICPs and cloned prospects. Once you have those profiles in hand, you're ready to bring creative into the mix and execute your marketing strategy.

What Do You Say to Your Leads and When Do You Say It?

Businesses in every sector have seen their customer base become more informed and proactive, but in B2B industries, the evolution from passive prospect to active information hunter has transformed the marketplace. With Google, review sites, and company blogs, discovering more about a product and the company that offers it is as quick as typing in a search string. Your business content has a lot to do with capturing the prospects that visit your website. But how do you prevent otherwise promising leads from bouncing away before they get to know all the facts you want them to learn about you? You constructed that picture during the discovery phase of the marketing cycle, and now it's time to put that knowledge to use. The next phase takes you from theory to execution, and lets your customers know more about you.

The chapters in Part III explore everything from the basics of outstanding email to the finer points of aiming at the moving SEO target. You'll understand more about how lead scoring contextualizes the data your Marketing AI gathered in the discovery phase and learn about best practices for major content streams; discover why personalization matters; and gain insight into using social media as a launch pad to help your marketing strategy soar. Perhaps most important, you'll find out how and when to deliver content that speaks to your audience to elicit a positive response.

Takeaways:

1. Marketing today is about connecting with relevant, compelling, engaging content and inviting your customers and prospects to learn enough about you to make a buying decision.
2. Quick access to big, accurate multisourced data is crucial to identifying your ICP and is very predictive of purchasing affinities, cross- and upsell opportunities, and retention strategies crucial to growing your business.
3. You can clone profitable new customers by using ICPs of your best customers to target and market to website visitors, third-party lists and online communities.

PART III

EXECUTION: RIGHT CONTENT, RIGHT PERSON, RIGHT TIME

CHAPTER 5

LEAD SCORING

A very important question is, how do you know when someone's ready to purchase? If you don't know where your leads are in your marketing pipeline, you can't meet their needs precisely. If you fail to meet their needs, a competitor will find a way. Lead scoring takes the data captured and appended to your MAI and frames it in terms of where each prospect is along the buying journey. With this contextualized view of your customers and their behavior, you learn who needs more information, what kind of information is correlated with a prospect's lifecycle stage and how best to deliver it. You'll also make your sales department more efficient and effective, because when a prospect reaches the sales-ready lead-score threshold, your marketing team hands off only fully nurtured sales-qualified leads.

It's useful to break scoring into three sections: demographic, behavioral, and contextual scores. Demographic scores, as their name suggests, include all the demographic and firmographic information you've amassed. These scores are derived from knowing who your audience is. Behavioral and contextual scoring is more fluid. Buyers' needs change, and these changes appear in their behavior as they interact with you. With your Marketing AI and a marketing team that knows how to harness its power, you're able to encode markers that track behavior across all your content, putting your leads' actions, interests, and decisions in context so the system can more accurately assess where they are in their buying journey.

Lead scoring is cumulative. As a lead's score rises to a given threshold, that lead rolls over to the next phase of the Lead Lifecycle. This cumulative score comes from all three lead-scoring elements (demographic, behavioral, and contextual), so a rise in one can trigger movement along the sales pipeline even if the others remain level. For example, a lead that starts off with markedly high demographic scores might be close to or above the marketing accepted lead threshold even before factoring in behavioral and contextual scores, indicating this lead is a close match to the firm's ICP.

Let's look at SEO Schematics as our example once again. The company has gathered enough data to create a cumulative lead-scoring framework that prioritizes leads in small companies within the advertising sector. Its best customers include business owners, CMOs and CIOs, so people with these job titles earn higher lead scores in the system. This demographic lead score is relatively stable over time.

The company's new Marketing AI has also pinpointed some interesting contextual trends. Leads that have viewed a pricing page on their website or downloaded case studies tend to be closer to a buying decision than visitors who viewed this information, and these leads therefore have a higher contextual score. Visitors who sign up for a webinar are highly correlated with sales, but those who follow through by attending are sending even stronger buying signals; these leads have higher contextual scores even as their demographic scores remain steady.

Lead scoring with the help of marketing automation tools gives businesses the power to rank and develop promising prospects. By taking a data-driven, analytical approach to lead scoring, companies maximize their marketing investments and get their leads sales-ready.

Establishing a Predeployment Baseline

When meteorologists model what weather systems might do, they use mountains of data from past events and compile probabilities based on the information they already have. Marketing AI systems use similar techniques to score leads and categorize them according to their potential value. Just as weather forecasts have gotten more accurate with the advent of satellite data and software that can analyze it, the science of lead scoring has progressed as technology and marketing automation software have improved.

Having a powerful, well-maintained CRM system is by far the most important factor in establishing a baseline for lead scoring. A CRM system can work in tandem with marketing automation systems or be a part of them, but a complete marketing automation system is more complex than a CRM system alone. A Marketing AI is artificial intelligence that cross-references, forms connections, and learns. While CRM has tremendous value for history and tracking, marketing automation software has far greater predictive power. A Marketing AI allows businesses to invest their time and effort precisely where and how they're most effective, and nowhere is that more important than with lead scoring.

The data your CRM system contains is the foundation of a sound lead-ranking strategy. Because you know the outcome of past leads, this data represents an important test case for your lead-scoring system. Feeding data about your past and current customers into the system lets you identify the areas in which these CRM profiles align so your lead scoring system can prioritize them. By calibrating your marketing automation system using data you already have, you get more accurate results. In classic spy thrillers the team synchronize watches so that every stage of its complex strategy unfolds according to plan. That's a bit like what calibrating your system using known data does for you. By modeling your lead-ranking strategy with information you already have, you test its veracity — one of the Vs of big data we talked about in Chapter 4. Lead scoring is a dynamic part of a marketing plan, not a static element. Over time, the contextual characteristics that define top leads can change. Competition, audience shifts, business growth, and industry changes impact how leads are valued, too, so marketing automation software that handles lead ranking must also be sensitive to external factors. Regular assessments allow companies to change with market shifts and to separate minor fluctuations from meaningful trends. The test and find out (TAFO) principle applies to developing your lead-scoring standards, and only a Marketing AI can keep up with the dynamics of changing customer needs, industry-wide events, and innovations.

In Chapter 4 you learned also about the lead types as defined by most marketing automation systems. We're going to be talking more about them here, so let's take another look at the Lead Lifecycle (Figure 5.1 — the diagram you first saw in the Prologue) and the Lead Lifecycle Model (Table 5.1), terms that define where your leads are in the sales pipeline:

Note how many of these stages of the buyer's journey rely on placing behavioral data in context. Your marketing-captured lead (MCL), for example, might evolve into marketing-qualified lead (MQL) status by going from visiting your site to signing up for your newsletter, a behavioral change that your Marketing AI can put into context as an important step toward sales readiness.

These terms will be familiar to you from the Lead Lifecycle diagram you first saw in the prologue. Figure 5.2 is another look at the chart with the lead types filled in:

See how the CRM synchs with the MAI at every step? That's part of the interdependence and vital stream of information that makes your

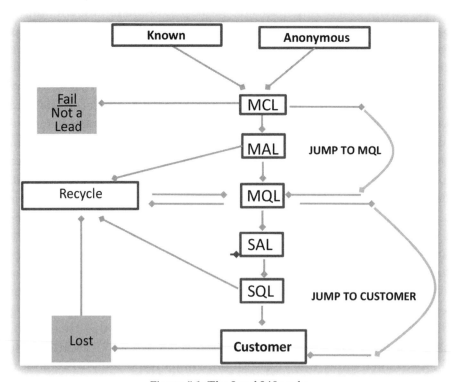

Figure 5.1: The Lead Lifecycle

CRM	CRM lead	A new lead from your CRM system.
ANYM	Anonymous	A prospect that has not yet shared its email address with you.
MCL	Marketing-Captured	A lead found you through SEO/SEM or other ways outside your CRM.
MAL	Marketing-Accepted (and Engaged)	A lead whose demographics meet the minimum criteria or are consistent with your Ideal Customer Profile. Engaged lead suggests active involvement with your site and brand via downloads and site visits.
MQL	Marketing-Qualified	A lead that has actively shared information with your marketing team and has a lead score high enough to warrant alerting the sales department.
SAL	Sales-Accepted	A lead that has been contacted by the sales team to establish BANT (budget, authority, need and timing) qualifications.
SQL	Sales-Qualified	A lead that is ready to become a customer but hasn't yet committed.
CLOSED WON	Customer	The end of your sales funnel but not the end of your marketing automation process.
JUNK	Unqualified	A lead that will never qualify. Competitors, employees, students, and incomplete or erroneous email address and contact information.
RECY	Recycle	Leads lacking the budget, authority, need and timing, or that need further nurturing to become clients.
CLOSED LOST	Lost Opportunity	An opportunity that was lost to your competitor. Recycle these leads in your marketing automation process.

Table 5.1: The Lead Lifecycle Model

Marketing AI fully responsive to contextual cues so it can perform as needed.

The Lead Lifecycle Rationale

In the beginning your prospects are just becoming aware that they may have a problem. This realization may be prompted by a promotional email they receive or through SEO and social links they click as they search for answers to perceived problems with their company's operations, growth, sales, or marketing. These are the top-of-funnel leads, those who are still anonymously searching through your website and may not yet have made themselves known by sharing their email address in

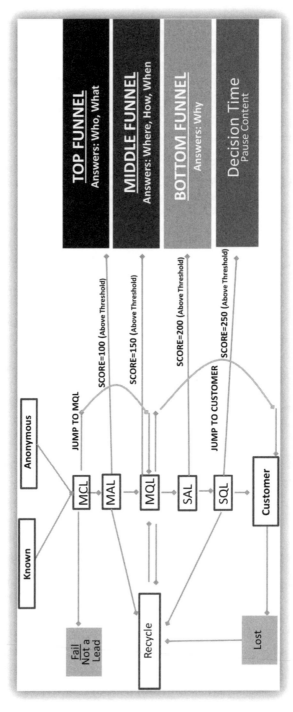

Figure 5.2: The Marketing AI Lead Lifecycle

return for gated content. Since there's not enough behavioral information about them, your AI's scoring at this level is based on their demographic profile. They're researching the "who" and "what" information they need to fix their problem. Serving the needs of prospects at this stage includes an appetizer of simple, bite-size content in blog posts, infographics, and newsletters.

Once these prospects confirm they have a problem, the next step is the Marketing Accepted Lead stage, where they learn "where," "when" and "how" they can find a solution. Here, the proper response from your Marketing AI is to serve them white papers, industry reports, and ROI calculators that help them discover possible solutions. This middle-of-funnel content should answer questions like "Where within my company/process, etc., can your product help me?"; "When do I start to see results?"; and "How does this work?"

As your prospects reach the Marketing Qualified Lead stage and just before leads are ready to be handed over to sales, your bottom-of-funnel content should promote the "why" of your message — why should they choose you in particular? Here, your pricing structure, case studies, video, and written testimonials should be sent to indelibly establish your value, and promotions aimed at differentiating you as the industry leader are key at this point.

Knowing when to send content is important, but it's just as vital to know when to stop. Your Marketing AI pauses the content stream (Figure 5.3) when sales-accepted leads become sales-qualified leads, because at that point any additional content could confuse and delay buyers' decisions to take the last few steps of that long journey. Potential customers don't need to know more details; they have already made a choice and need marketing messages to step out of the way while the sale happens. A Marketing AI controls this delicate, but critical shift from marketing to sales and back to marketing.

Live Deployment of Lead-Scoring Strategies

After calibrating your lead-scoring system and defining your leads' taxonomy, your Marketing AI is ready to receive new data with which it can monitor engagement, can assess buying readiness and can deliver both

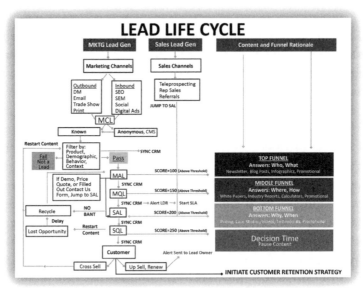

Figure 5.3: The Lead Lifecycle Sales Funnel

cumulative and contextual rankings to help your marketing team prioritize its efforts.

The BANT model uses four elements to determine readiness to buy. Only when these four key factors are favorable do promising leads become customers, but taking too long to assess BANT readiness gives competitors an opportunity to contact and develop *your* lead. Marketing automation and lead scoring are designed to use demographic scoring and behavioral activity to serve content that will reduce the time and distance between initial contact and lead development. Software tools that help establish a prospect's budget, pinpoint the person with buying authority, locate needs, and monitor a lead's timeline throughout the sales process have modernized the BANT concept, bringing it into the 21st century. BANT plays a direct role in lead scoring, but it also underlies many other measurable characteristics in indirect ways. Job titles, for example, correlate closely with buying authority and affect a lead's score, but recent and frequent clicks on your content demonstrate a high level of need and proper timing.

Lead-scoring systems use both intrinsic characteristics and behaviors to map and rank prospects. Data from an existing CRM system can provide much of the raw material for initial lead scoring, but important information can also come from surveys, preference pages, or data enhancement through append services. For behavioral data, a marketing automation system that tracks every aspect of a lead across multiple marketing channels is a must.

The following sections detail some of the primary sources of information that lead-ranking systems use to generate their scores.

Demographic and Firmographic Lead Scoring Elements — Explicit Ranking Data
Some facts, such as the information in the list below, speak volumes about a lead's likelihood of further development. Demographic and firmographic information tells a lead-scoring system how closely a lead fits the company's ICP. This explicit data is the foundation on which a lead-ranking strategy rests, and it's vital to ensure that the information here is accurate. Marketing automation systems can update this data regularly.

- Job title
- Role (function)
- Budget
- Purchasing authority (decision maker, researcher, part of a team?)
- Honors and awards
- Certifications and degrees
- Years of experience
- Preferred email platform
- Company size
- Company revenue
- Social network participation
- Professional group affiliations
- Location, including city, state and ZIP
- Lead source

Behavior-Based Lead Scoring Elements — Implicit Ranking Data
How leads behave is highly correlated with their level of need and timing. That's why it's important for your Marketing AI to keep a separate, cumulative-behavioral score.

Marketing automation software tracks how a lead interacts with your website, social- media presence, emails, and other online marketing channels via anonymous browser cookies and JavaScript applets to build a clear picture of where that lead is in the sales cycle. This implicit data is highly predictive of how leads will behave in the future. Look closely at successful results, the interactions and behaviors that prospects took along the way to becoming customers, and you'll see that certain content is highly correlated with conversions. Some of these behaviors include downloading white papers, visiting pricing pages, and attendance at webinars. Understanding past behavior and knowing what your potential customers need to become buyers allows your AI to act on the cues these leads provide. Context determines content.

Think of online behavior as digital body language marketers can use to determine what leads need to develop. In a face-to-face conversation, you can readily gauge your audience's interest and judge whether it really wants to hear more or is just being polite. How do you know? You read subtle cues without even consciously knowing it. Your Marketing AI gives you the power to gauge interest and adapt even when your conversation takes place simultaneously with millions of prospects in a global context. Marketing automation places behavioral cues in context for you, and by contextualizing that information, you're able to communicate naturally with each and every one of your leads.

Below are some of the behavioral cues we look for when gauging where leads are in the marketing pipeline and ranking their sales readiness. As implicit information helps your MAI assess interest, it's absolutely essential to monitor and score.

- Requests for samples or free trials
- Newsletter subscriptions
- Pricing Pages
- Hand raise (contact us) forms
- Past buying habits
- Attendance of live-streamed events
- Information downloads
- Email opens and clicks

- Seminar or webinar attendance
- Recency and frequency of site visits
- Social referrals, retweets, likes, etc.

Contextual scoring is based on the lead's category of interest. Most companies sell multiple products and understanding which product your lead is most interested in is critical to your ability to maximize relevance in your messaging. Your lead will tell you everything you need to know, but if you aren't observing and cataloging their behaviors, you will probably miss your golden opportunity to close the deal.

Negative Results as Lead Ranking Elements

Sometimes prospects say more with what they don't do than what they do. To go back to the body language analogy, these signals would be equivalent to a stifled yawn or a look around the room from a conversation partner. Lead-scoring systems can assign negative numbers, in some cases, to move these leads down the list of priorities. Lead scoring should also build in a natural decay-scoring strategy for leads that no longer interact with you over a given period of time.

Some examples include:

- Joining a do-not-call list
- Long periods of website inactivity (lost opportunity, changed jobs)
- High bounce rates
- Unsubscribe requests from email and newsletters
- Deleting email messages unread
- Spam complaints
- Lack of response to telemarketing or email
- Negative comments on social media or blog posts

Sample Lead Scoring Results

Quantifying leads according to their explicit data fit and implicit engagement looks different from system to system, but generally, lead-ranking software can generate a detailed report on how every lead's score is calculated. Your pre-deployment baseline sets the criteria for evaluation, but with most lead-scoring software, each element should be further adjusted (individually) for fine-tuning.

The following example represents what MAS lead-scoring software may generate for SEO Schematics (reasons for the scores are in parenthetical notes).

Explicit Data:

Company president	+15	(High authority equals high lead value)
Advertising-related SIC code	+10	(Many of SEO Schematics' customers are in advertising)
Ideal customer profile	+20	(Extra points for meeting title, industry, and size ICPs)
MS in computer engineering	+ 7	(Technical knowledge aligns well with current CRM base)
50+ employees	+ 5	(Company size is a good fit for target market)
Active on social media	+ 5	(Social media activity correlates closely with sales)
Location 100–200 miles	+ 2	(A closer business would have a higher score here)

Behavioral Data:

Webinar download	+20	(Participants have historically been close to buying)
Newsletter subscription	+15	(Newsletter readers are highly engaged)
Visited pricing page	+10	(A visit to the pricing page indicates high interest)
Time on site >5 minutes	+ 7	(More time at the site implies more engagement)
No response to telemarketing	- 5	(This lead's interest doesn't extend to phone calls)

Total score: **91**

This lead is a close fit with the company's customer profile and has evinced a high level of interest; it's sales-ready and needs very little incentive to go from prospect to customer. The lowest marks relate to the company's distance from the seller and the negative response to telemarketing. Knowing these details, the marketing team can then come up with strategies to lessen the potential impact of distance on this sale (offering 24/7 customer assistance via phone or website, for example) and to contact this customer by means other than his office phone.

Automated lead scoring also categorizes leads into priority levels. The example above would be an A-list priority due to the high overall score and few negatives. The A group might include any lead score above 60; the B group could range from 30 to 60, and the C-list includes those from 0 to 30. Leads scores should never be set below zero, because you want to give a lead that's built up significant negative behavior the ability to score positively if it presents a real opportunity in the future. But you should consider adding a recycling phase or reducing its score to zero, particularly if that lead had chosen to opt out of available marketing channels.

Postdeployment Lead-Ranking Analysis and Optimization

An automated lead-scoring system can crunch huge numbers, but its results appear in an easily read format. A graph of lead scores (Figure 5.4) indicates the next steps your marketing team should take to capitalize on each lead's unique characteristics.

While scoring systems are customizable and can translate results into multiple formats, graphs along an X-Y axis are becoming the industry standard. If the X axis represents demographic fit and the Y axis indicates behavior, leads naturally fall into four quadrants.

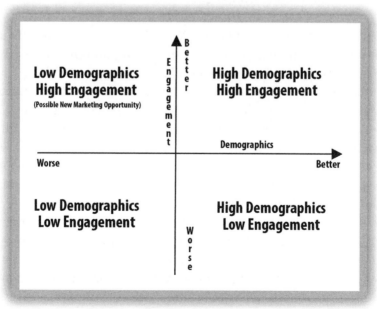

Figure 5.4: Lead Ranking Analysis Report

1. Those with a good demographic fit and high engagement scores are at the upper right of the graph and are your highest priority. They are on the verge of buying and can often go directly to the sales team to close.

2. Leads with a good fit but low engagement appear at the bottom right of the graph and represent long-term investments. Although they may not be customers yet, they have a good likelihood of becoming buyers in the future with the right marketing messages over time.

3. The data points in the upper left quadrant of your graph represent the outsiders, leads with high engagement scores but don't look like your current customers demographically. These leads can either be your competitors, employees and students, or these leads can indicate an untapped new market that deserves further study. Your marketing team should contact these leads and learn more about them to find out more about their interest.

4. At the lower left are leads with low engagement and an unlikely fit. Their lead scores are the lowest and indicate that they are the lowest priority for your marketing department. As with all leads, they may change over time, but they should not be the focus of a major marketing campaign.

Lead scoring is a moving target. As leads take new actions, their profiles and scores can change, so your marketing automation tools must keep pace with these changes by regularly updating files. Data updates may be automatic, but you can take additional steps to maximize the power and precision of lead ranking through analysis and review.

Look at your results over time to pinpoint wins and losses. If high-scoring leads fail to result in sales, it's vital to understand why. These cases are often the most instructive, so scrutinize them carefully to see if they represent cases of poorly qualified leads finding their way through the system or well qualified ones that the conversion process failed before the promising lead reached the sales department. Is there a way to account for similar cases in the future by adjusting the information measured or sensitivity of your lead scoring system?

Demographic and firmographic data is probably a part of your CRM system already, but the rich vein of information about behavior is something an automated marketing system is particularly good at mining. A thorough nurturing campaign is the essential ingredient that supports sales by maximizing the profitability of every lead. A lead without scoring is an unknown; if neither your marketing department nor your sales team can provide accurate information on the lead, it will remain unqualified.

A mismanaged or siloed scoring system that fails to take demographic, behavioral, and contextual information into account will likewise not produce good results. Even if you have a lead-scoring system that tells you where a lead is now, if the system is unable to track prospects over time and assign them to nurture tracks that make sense for them you can't become part of the solution. Without the right nurture campaign to send the right content at the right time, you're wasting your efforts and your leads' time. Look at behavioral data over time to fine-tune lead scoring and develop a more accurate picture of prospects as they interact with you.

It's tempting for creative to take an idea and run with it during the execution phase, pushing it out of the nest and watching it fly, but without a blueprint in place and the necessary strategy to hold the concept aloft, your Marketing AI cannot execute a successful campaign. No matter how artful a creative effort is it can only succeed if it reaches the right audience with the right message at the right time through their preferred marketing channels. In Chapter 6, you'll learn how to coordinate content across multiple channels and guide your prospects to where they need to go to turn cold to warm prospects and opportunities into satisfied customers.

Takeaways:

1. A Marketing AI uses a combination of demographic, behavioral, and contextual scores to track your leads' actions, interests, and decisions in context so the system can assess and serve the right content based on where they are in their buying journey.
2. Use the outcome of past leads from your CRM system to calibrate the predictive capability of your lead-scoring system.
3. Use the Lead Ranking Analysis Report (Figure 5.4) to compare the prospects you're generating with the ideal demographic and engagement score. Your goal is to align your marketing to generate as many of your prospects in the top right quadrant as possible.

CHAPTER 6

INITIAL COMMUNICATION, RETARGETING, AND TRIGGERS

The Internet has caused a paradigm shift in the way buyers gain information about your products, services, and company before they ever get in touch with you. You receive a huge advantage when you gain control over communications timing. The "when" of approaching your customers is as important as the "how." You wouldn't ask someone to marry you on your first date, and the same holds true for customer relationships. You also don't want to ignore the chance to affect a lead's buying decision with the right words at the right time. Those moments are often fleeting, and missing them is an opportunity cost few businesses can afford. In this chapter we'll look at how to approach your prospects, how to respond to their behavioral triggers, and how to retarget them so you retain as many potential customers as possible.

By now you understand that the real power of behavioral targeting is its predictive capability. You learn what your customers are doing now, and use that information to tell you what future leads will do when they encounter the same triggers. Capturing behavioral and contextual data shows you the decisive points along a buyer's journey so you can position effective content at those turning points. Think about your customers' buying DNA (Chapter 3) as biological switches that direct how stem cells develop. You're taking an active role in your customers' choices with triggers and retargeting.

Responsive marketing is smart marketing. Over time, your email campaigns become increasingly agile and better able to predict how new leads will respond, making every campaign smarter than the last. This evolutionary process can't happen with conventional email service providers (ESP) and siloed software systems, because they aren't equipped to process and link behavioral data with other elements of your marketing strategy and contextualize it. Context is a cornerstone of marketing automation and the foundation of your Marketing AI.

Before you send the first email and introduce yourself to new leads, you need to map out exactly what you hope to accomplish with your campaign. Every business wants to grow, earn more profits, and get more customers. You have to map a specific set of goals with your creative team and Marketing AI experts working together. With your MAS, you're able to outline your reasons for contacting your customers with every communication; when everything you do has a purpose, you achieve far greater success.

You should ask why it's important for you to send this email or post that banner, what you want to communicate to your newest subscribers, and what do you do about your most loyal customers or those who haven't connected with you in a while. Marketing automation coordinates all these purposeful connections for you and helps your marketing efforts evolve into a strategic rather than a logistic process. Some possible reasons and goals for making contact may include:

- Attracting new prospects
- Engaging your audience
- Displaying your thought leadership
- Influencing trends
- Producing interest and desire
- Finding new subscribers
- Alerting new prospects to an offer in exchange for information
- Selling products and services
- Establishing or expanding customer loyalty programs
- Seeking referrals
- Producing site registrants
- Generating whitepaper/webinar sign ups
- Creating greater brand awareness

Once you know what you want to say, it's time to think about how you say it.

Initial Communications — Have Them at Hello

How do you introduce yourself to new prospects or bring new ideas to current customers? Those initial communications are critical to your current campaign's success, but they also play a major role in brand perception, data acquisition, and future contacts. Your initial communication may be widespread and diffuse, such as with television ads, radio spots, video, and website banners. It may be intensely focused and deep, as with direct mail, email, telemarketing, and social media channels. You and your marketing team use your Marketing AI to develop a blueprint that emphasizes one or another aspect of your initial communication strategy. Of all your initial contact avenues, though, email is usually the star of the show, and for good reason.

Email as an Initial Communication

Nothing approaches email for rapidity, low cost, and size of available universe. It's also the most trackable method of communication you have, generating mountains of useful data in easy-to-analyze formats. Marketing automation specialists and data-governance managers love email as a primary communication tool because it's simple to test and tweak. That's good news because email is often the foundation on which the rest of your marketing blueprint sits. It's critical for marketers to get email right, because the data it generates will govern the direction of future campaigns and retargeting efforts.

Although it's easy to use, email is also easy to misuse without good data curation. You learned in Chapter 3 how vital data hygiene is and how lost opportunities and irrelevant advertising can cost you. Successful email marketers give customers information they want, but first, they have to figure out how best to deliver that content while keeping your company's name clean in the eyes of ISPs.

Email's ascendancy as a marketing tool is assured, and the trend is ever upward. Today, smart phones and mobile devices have surpassed the use of computers as the preferred access to the Internet. This paradigm shift directly affects how you communicate with your customers, making responsive email design a must. More people read their email on mobile devices than on desktop systems. Your customers are no longer tethered to their desks when they read your correspondence, so email that's short, concise, and responsive fits the mobile-first mentality. That's already enough to make email a central part of your marketing blueprint, and in successive chapters you'll learn how to execute those email strategies to maximize conversions.

Direct Mail

People have multiple email addresses (not all of which are useful for B2B marketing, which should go exclusively to corporate addresses), but they typically have only one corporate business address at a time. Direct mail as an initial communication channel is a costlier proposition than email, and is therefore an optimal retargeting channel, but if you're working from a clean list (Chapter 3) it's a potentially effective way to reach a highly localized audience. For many companies, direct mail makes sense because it's a relatively unspoiled channel, particularly for B2B companies. With fewer competitors, your voice stands out, especially when your message is closely tailored to your prospects' interests, thanks to your MAI. Your marketing team can also find ways to save on direct mail, including ride-alongs that double up on mailing by enclosing multiple items in a single envelope; using digital printing services; and investing in high-quality mailing lists.

Your MAS plays a key role in making direct mail work both as an introductory marketing channel and as part of a long-term lead nurturing campaign. With it, you're able to target your campaign regions with far finer granularity than with any other direct mail software system. Combined with the other demographic and firmographic information you've discovered through the system's data append and enhancement tools, you can fine-tune mailings to reach your ICP and make such campaigns viable from the outset. For B2B industries that are (necessarily) regionally restricted, such as commercial-property management firms and corporate architects, direct mail could send a strong signal of quality as an initial point of contact.

Banner Advertising

With the right data analysis and a careful host selection behind it, banner advertising can be an effective initial communication tool, especially if you're aiming for a high number of impressions on a single spend. The key to using banner advertising well is in matching the banner to the audience, a task that's ideal for Marketing AI, with its multidimensional view across marketing channels. If you sell cleaning supplies for food-service industries, for example, your banner ad will thrive on local and regional restaurant journals, but won't gain much traction on a gourmet-food blog. Banners can be an important part of an integrated marketing campaign as a way to increase familiarity. Ad-blocking software on users' computers, especially when they visit a site from the office, can be a limiting factor for the efficacy of banner ads, but their low price and ease of production still make them a valuable part of your marketing blueprint.

Marketing automation systems excel at serving the right content to the right audience. Moreover, they can track behavior on a deeper level than click-throughs, giving you important information about time spent on the source page, responses to A/B split testing, (a topic we'll cover in Chapter 16), and the interrelation of all this data with existing customer information. By contextualizing how people interact with your banners and your brand, your MAI is able to give you a far more complete picture of leads and what they want most from you.

Social Media

Like email messages, social media networks are excellent as a low- or no-cost way of raising your prospects' awareness and building essential mindshare. Because it takes only a small time investment to build a social media profile, connect with users, and participate in the conversation with your customers, social media should be a part of every marketing campaign. However, relying too heavily on social media is like building a house on shifting sands: It's ideal for initial contact and retargeting efforts, but it's not intended to rule your marketing plan.

A MAS puts social media channels in context, linking them in meaningful, relevant ways to customized content. A link in your Twitter feed to a single page can serve different customers different context, thanks to personal URLs and tracking cookies. If, for example, SEO Schematics wanted to invite customers to read its latest blog post, the graphics and banners surrounding the post change depending on who clicked through to read it.

Content Marketing

Although you'll read much more about content marketing and native advertising in Chapter 7, it's worth a mention here because it's so vital to your marketing success. Leaving room in your marketing budget and timeline for content is non-negotiable. Good SEO also counts as a form of initial communication, because it's the first way many people will find you via a web search or backlink from another source. It's never too early to start thinking about content, but during the blueprint phase, keep those content ideas broad and flexible.

Remember, more than half of your customers come to you with some knowledge about you, not all of which comes directly from you. Your content is your contribution to the conversation, letting your leads get a better idea of who you are as a brand. Marketing automation is ferociously content-hungry — it has to be, because it serves so many people a customized experience. That means you need to have sufficient content variety for every audience segment at every stage of your buyers' journey, from anonymous lead to customer. Your Marketing AI coordinates all that content and ensures that your initial contact via content marketing fits what your leads need to know.

Retargeting — Hello Again

Retargeting and reengagement using tracking pixels, or MAS integration with third parties' retargeting firms, gives your Marketing AI another bite at the apple by letting you follow up on an initial contact.

Currently, your Marketing AI has access to two types of retargeting: JavaScript or cookie-based and list-based methods.

JavaScript-Based Retargeting

The first priority for you when an anonymous lead visits is to get an email address so you can contact that lead directly. JavaScript or cookie-based retargeting (sometimes referred to as pixel tracking) is much more than a method for redisplaying your material to an anonymous site visitor. The conversion strategy begins when an anonymous visitor is taken to a specific page on your website that sets the cookie. When that visitor leaves your site to surf the web, the cookie signals the retargeting firms to begin serving contextually specific ads showing products displayed on visited web pages. A smart strategy here is to gain the prospect's email address by inviting the prospect to fill out a landing page form in return for valuable content.

List-Based Retargeting

Third-party retargeting companies and social networks such as Facebook, LinkedIn, and Twitter offer marketing programs that match your prospects' email addresses to their members, then serve up HTML or text-based ads to prospects you select from your database. These prospects are selected by your MAI based on their Lead Lifecycle stage, taking into account demographic, behavioral, and contextual scores that have the highest potential value or propensity to respond.

When you retarget people you've previously reached with an initial communication, you can expand on that brief initial contact and win more conversions as prospects hear the rest of the story. Retargeting works because it's contextually relevant. Because you can serve up graphics and copy to a lead displaying the exact products and services that originally brought the prospect to your website, you enjoy higher customer-retention rates and give a boost to your acquisition results. A successful retargeting campaign can double or triple the power of the initial marketing campaign by reengaging with customers who opened your email or clicked through, but didn't act or who added an item to a shopping cart without buying. It can also be a powerful strategy that wins your company mindshare when a prospect is evaluating competitors during the decision stage. Staying in a lead's consciousness and establishing your organization as the industry leader can convince him to buy from you.

Marketing departments spend a remarkable amount of time and effort earning clicks and conversions, but without contextualized retargeting, they could be losing a larger chunk of that investment than necessary. With retargeting, you take your message to another format, extend another invitation to your prospects, and convince uncertain prospects and customers that now is the time to act. Marketing AI prepares you for retargeting even before your campaign launches. With a retargeting strategy in place before the first email or banner ad goes out, you retain as many connections as possible with your leads, and greater connectedness means higher conversion rates.

Building retargeting into your marketing efforts is critical to maximizing your ROIs. Instead of thinking of it as a failsafe or fallback strategy, build it into the main body of your marketing plan. Here, an effective three-step retargeting strategy:

Step 1: Reengagement — Give fence sitters a little nudge over the top with communications that build on the previous message. For example, you might follow an offer that includes a free subscription with a targeted email that includes a start-my-free-subscription-now button. Contextually linking your retargeting efforts with recent communications reinforces the message and brings it to top of mind again for your prospects.

Step 2: Personalization — If your first contact with a prospect gave you new data about her, make your next communication personalized to encourage an ongoing customer relationship. If, for example, a visitor to your e-commerce site registered with information that his company is in the advertising industry, your response might include industry-specific personalization in the title: "SEO Ranking Secrets for Advertising Agencies." A message is only as personalized as your knowledge of the person receiving it, and it goes deeper than simply using a name. Communicate context-rich details you've learned at each step along the Lead Lifecycle to foster two-way interaction and to boost conversion rates after retargeting. Other potential triggers for personalization include job function, new data on interests, and new product launches, all of which can add context and dimension to your conversation with leads.

Step 3: Last-chance offers — At some point prospects who aren't interested in this campaign should drop out of its retargeting efforts, but don't let it happen without a final message to remind them of your offer.

An important note: Cutting your losses on this campaign with a last-chance message doesn't mean you remove those prospects from your overall database; just because they aren't interested in this offer at this time doesn't mean the next campaign won't result in a big sale.

Reengagement Strategies

No matter how tempting your offer may be, your audience will respond to it in one of three ways: with enthusiasm, with uncertainty, or with a shrug. Promising leads range from interested to eager, and they're prime candidates for retargeting with more details on an initial offer. Thanks to your MAS lead-scoring system, you'll know which is which and understand precisely how to approach these leads with the appropriate content for their position within the Lead Lifecycle. Make it easy for them to act, and they'll do the rest. For uncertain responses from leads that are still at the top of the sales funnel, more information could be the deciding factor that results in action. Even leads that have expressed little interest in a given offer can still be retargeted with a quick message to alert them that the offer is ending soon.

Email and direct mail are viable ways to retarget potential customers, but don't overlook telemarketing, an avenue of reengaging that has a high success rate when implemented well. The key to making telemarketing work well is relevance. A high lead score indicates high relevance, so by calling only the leads that have the highest scores, you make the best use of your retargeting resources. If customers have already expressed some interest in talking more with you about an offer, then a call is often a deciding factor when making a coordinated, relevant marketing effort. Using a clean database and working with a marketing company that knows how to manage telemarketing campaigns is a must. We discuss the new role of telemarketing in an AI-driven marketing strategy in Chapter 11.

By defining your reengagement strategy prior to execution, your Marketing AI takes the guesswork out of the process when it's crunch time. Establish your multitouch strategy during this stage using the built-in tools marketing automation software offers. Once you've deployed your initial email campaign and generated your pulse, a re-engagement blueprint helps you know how to monitor it and keep it strong, how to know which triggers create a cascade of additional events, and how to work toward the positive outcomes. Ideal reengagement efforts draw on what you learned from the initial campaign and retain a common thread in the creative, content, and tone, and typically kick up the urgency and utilize additional distribution channels. Following are five re-engagement strategies that excel:

1. **Direct mail** – Send a tailored direct mail piece that is delivered only to those who opened the email but didn't convert. This is a much more qualified audience worthy of the higher expenses associated with direct mail.

2. **Banner advertising** – Reinforce your message to everyone who opened the initial email as they move on with their day and venture online is a strong tactic that keeps your brand in front of mind and can lead to a returned visitor and eventual conversion.

3. **Telemarketing** – Often overlooked, telemarketing offers great one-to-one interaction that can provide just the necessary nudge to convert that warm prospect into your next customer. A strong retargeting campaign via telemarketing also lets your marketing team gather some critical intel as to how your target audience perceives your product or service.

4. **Landing page** – Yes, you can use your site to retarget an email recipient. When customers have clicked on your email link, you can cookie their browsers and retarget them specifically as they visit other sites in your efforts to win them back and convert them.

5. **Triggered email** – This is an especially effective method that deserves more explanation, and you'll learn more about it in Chapter 9, as well as in this chapter.

Triggers and Flows

Industry analysts have noticed tectonic shifts in successful email marketing efforts. While other aspects of email enhance open rates, including subject lines, subheaders, and "from" lines, one of the biggest factors in improving opens and click-to-open ratios is whether the email was triggered. Triggered messages aren't sent at random; they go out in response to some action from the intended recipient. For example, your marketing team might have automated welcome messages lined up to send to customers who subscribe to an online magazine or thank-you messages to those who've just made a purchase. Time triggers could go out on birthdays, company founding dates or "win backs" after a certain period of inactivity to encourage prospects to return.

How much of a difference does triggered email make? According to current benchmarks, triggered messaging has a 75 percent higher open rate and a 115 percent higher click rate over conventional campaigns. With a large email campaign, those numbers could translate into staggering increases in conversion rates. Despite that major incentive, most marketing companies haven't yet capitalized on triggered email messaging. By achieving greater relevance and specificity, triggered email creates a level of engagement that few other channels can match. Think about what you know of the importance of behavioral data in providing context, and you start to see the tremendous power of triggered email as part of a logical flow through the marketing pipeline.

Journalists consider who, what, when, where, why, and how when reporting a story. You already know how important it is to establish who you are, who your customers are, and what you say to one another. The logistics — the how and where of data discovery and analytics — are already in place with marketing automation. At the beginning of this chapter, we talked about the importance of when. Triggered emails set up in your MAS are a big part of maintaining the tempo of your campaign, organizing the timing for you. It's the ideal tool for managing time-sensitive elements of your campaign — and it's almost all time-sensitive, so that's a tall order.

Flow charts establish a sequence for carrying out a process or making a decision, and marketing automation flows serve a similar purpose. They trace trajectories of leads through your pipeline and recalculate the best possible path with each decision your prospects take. As with flow charts, some paths are longer than others. If a prospect comes to you already asking about prices and delivery dates, your Marketing AI spots these signals and identifies this potential customer as a highly motivated lead, alerting sales right away to get this buyer in as an SAL or SQL (sales-accepted or sales-qualified lead; see the Lead Lifecycle figure in Chapter 5). Other routes are circuitous, going through a lengthy nurturing process across multiple channels. Especially in B2B, where individual buyers are rarely the sole decision-makers, and need volumes of information before making a choice, establishing a good flow is essential to lead nurturing.

Flows are something you and your marketing automation specialists build, but the movement through them is controlled by customer actions. They aren't prescriptive; you aren't giving orders to your leads out of context, but you are suggesting courses of action to them based on behavioral cues. Paying attention to these triggers and refining flows by modifying them according to the data your Marketing AI collects is as much of a benefit to your buyers as it is to you. They get what they need when they need it, and you get a fully realized revenue-marketing upgrade.

Tips and Tricks for Triggers

A single email message can be powerful, but additional messages that go out in response to actions your prospect takes are even more effective for eliciting a response. You may send triggered emails to remind a prospective customer about items left in a shopping cart and never checked out or to make contact again after a set length of time without getting in touch. To make the most of triggered email, keep the following guidelines in mind, and tailor your triggers to events that are relevant to your clientele.

Personalize — Personalized emails always have more of an impact than generic messages, and that's true for triggered email, too. Birthday coupons are a common example of personalizing triggered messages, especially in B2C contexts, but they're far from your only option. Changes to a prospect's status on preference pages can be useful triggers too. Someone who changes "Miss" to "Mrs." or updates an address with a new ZIP code presents a new opportunity for triggered email. For B2B industries, changes to job title or updates to the personal information linked to a pre-existing job title represent opportunity; not only do you maintain your contact with the individual who used to sit at a particular desk, you also get a chance to reach out to the person who sits there now. Whenever data changes, your MAS can respond to it with a triggered message.

Create a Connection — Whenever possible, tie the triggered mail both to the event that triggered it and to a customer's current needs. For example, SEO Schematics offers a webinar. The flow action starts with an emailed invitation. Those that sign up are immediately sent a confirmation with a link that automates a calendar function to insert the date and time of the webinar in the prospect's Outlook. Two days later, the flow action sends those that haven't yet signed up an email alerting them that there are only a few seats left for the webinar. On the day of the webinar, the flow action sends an email reminder to the sign ups 15 minutes before the start of the webinar. The final flow steps check to see who attended and send a thanks-for-attending email to the attendees, and a sorry-you-couldn't-attend note to the no-shows, along with a link to a video recast of the webinar. By connecting the trigger at both ends — that is, serving the customer's needs as well as addressing the triggering event — you delight your prospect and forge stronger links between you and your customer.

Use Multiple Data Sources — Data enhancement is critical to maximizing the utility of triggered emails. With a more complete customer profile, you're able to choose from a wider range of possible triggers and find which ones bring the highest response rates. If all you know is your recipient's place of business, you have relatively few options; add in key characteristics such as job title, buying authority, company size, and role, and you have a wealth of additional options for reaching that customer with triggered email. The more you know, the more potential trigger points your Marketing AI can identify and act on, dramatically increasing response rates.

Be Patient — The point of triggered automated email is that you don't have to micromanage it. Once you've set up your triggers, you can focus on other aspects of your integrated marketing strategy while the system does the work. That means you can set triggers for weeks or even months away, allowing you to reintroduce yourself to recipients on a larger timescale. If you were to rely on manual email blasts, some of your best leads could be lost; with automated email triggers, that isn't an issue. You can afford to be patient.

Direct Your Prospects — Triggered email still needs a strong call to action and a direct purpose. Making the reason for your email clear and putting your call to action (CTA) above the fold is even more important with triggered messages because it's a reaction, not just a connection. An introductory email or sales message has a little more room to expand; a triggered email should be brief, concise and tightly focused on the event that made it happen.

Nurturing Strategies with Triggered Email

To get a clearer idea of how flows work and what they mean to a marketing campaign, let's look at how SEO Schematics has its email flow coordinated. This is a simplified version of flows that looks only at email marketing and only at the uppermost level of flow construction. Marketing AI systems are powerful and allow for more nuanced, sophisticated flows, but as each system is different, it's useful to look at a simplified model that's representative of the concept.

Introductions — Welcome Series

Whenever a prospective customer visits the SEO Schematics site, asks for information, or downloads content for the first time, that lead enters the welcome flow. In its first email, marketing automation team members give prospects a brief overview of who the company is and what it can do for them. Using its new marketing automation tools, the company has great data to use for personalization. Writing slightly different content for people who enter the welcome series of emails through different paths can go a long way toward making readers feel valued.

Possible triggers for welcome emails could include visiting your site, subscribing to your newsletter, and joining your forum or blog community. Typically, you'll set up the first autoresponder welcome email immediately after getting your prospect's email address. It's often a good practice to include a registration link in this initial email to ensure you have the right address.

"Is There Anything Else?" – Request Series

Visits to a pricing page, downloads, and emailed questions should divert the flow of triggered emails from welcoming readers to serving their needs as prospective customers. They're much farther along the sales pipeline than new visitors to the site, so the triggered email should likewise be more in-depth. These prospects already have a pretty good idea what the company is and what it does; they just need some key details filled in to make their buying decision simpler. Content at this stage should ease that phase change from guest to promising prospect.

Because potential customers tend to spend more time in the fact-finding phase of their relationship than in other phases, you may have multiple triggers at this point (as SEO Schematic did). You want different email going out to the people who are moving rapidly through your sales pipeline than the message going out to people who have slowed or stopped their progress. For example, you might have one flow for people who have requested a quote, another for those who have downloaded an industry related report, and yet another for those who abandoned their shopping cart or wish list.

Fill 'Em Up – Replacement Series

This series of triggered emails go out to customers and help with retention rather than acquisition. Because SEO Schematics needs to update software for its customers regularly to keep on top of search engines' algorithm changes, the company has set email triggers to remind buyers of that. Anything customers come back to buy merits its own email cascade that triggers automatically when clients purchase these items or upgrades. Calibrating the timing on these letters is essential; when they're timed well, recipients consider them a courtesy, but if they come too soon or too late, they're ignored. Sales records tell the company most of what it needs to know to time these messages just right.

Welcome Back – Reactivation Series

SEO Schematics values every customer. When one of its longtime clients disappears, they want a way to reestablish contact. With data appending, they're able to track more of their former clients, so now they want to set up a reactivation flow to make it easy for these former clients to re-enter the sales pipeline.

Even your best customers sometimes go dormant without any reason you can see. A triggered email can sometimes be enough to remind them they'd like to see more of you too. You can set this series to trigger as a contingency plan that most customers won't ever see unless they go dormant for a while. Depending on your customers' usual time from first contact to sale, you might set this cascade in motion after anything from a few weeks to a few months.

We've talked about the when of establishing contact with your customers. In Chapter 7 you'll gain an in-depth perspective on what you want to say once you have their attention through a compelling initial communication and ongoing nurture campaign. We'll start with one of the hottest topics in digital marketing today — content marketing.

Takeaways:

1. Triggered messages sent in response to actions taken by your prospect are the most effective at eliciting a positive response.
2. Use reengagement strategies to target prime candidates with appropriate content for their position in the Lead Lifecycle.
3. You build flow charts...but customers control their movement through them.

CHAPTER 7

CONTENT

The sales pipeline is no longer a straight shot from your first impression to closing a sale. Potential customers now educate themselves, and they come to you knowing a great deal about you. Typically, your leads now are 50 to 80 percent more educated about your product/service and the market prior to speaking with anyone in your organization. Content marketing lets you control that education by building the knowledge base your prospects use to learn about you and providing thought leadership that builds trust in your brand. Thought leadership demonstrates your company's contribution to best practices, helps leads make informed choices, and gives customers a reason to buy from you instead of the competition.

"Content is king." You'll find that phrase in almost every marketing article or book that discusses content marketing, but it isn't really an accurate metaphor. It leaves out one of the most important aspects of content. When people stay on your website to read a feature-length article, take action on your landing page, or subscribe to your newsletter, they're essentially casting a vote. Content isn't king; it's democratically elected.

With that in mind, what can you do to get your audience's vote, win its support? People vote with their feet. If they don't find what they like from your competitors, they'll come to you — and you have to be ready to deliver. In this chapter you'll find out how to earn your prospects' votes by learning how to get an audience interested, build authority, gather vital customer data, eliminate duplication, generate leads, and retain valued customers with your content marketing.

Your Marketing AI is instrumental in every aspect of your content marketing strategy. With it, you coordinate cross-channel content seamlessly, pinpoint exactly where each prospect's interest lies by analyzing contextual data, and deliver precisely the right information at the right time according to your prospects' position on the Lead Lifecycle. You're able to customize content to an unprecedented degree, giving your future customers all the information they need to make buying decisions organically, instead of relying on advertising alone.

A powerful MAI also quantifies how well your content-marketing strategy is working in ways that other tools can't manage. Conventional analytics are not well equipped to measure ROI on content-based revenue marketing. Older tools give feedback about search terms or bounce rates, but they can't track more sophisticated metrics, such as the revenue contributions of each channel, the most effective landing page design, or lead-scoring priorities that point the way to your future top customers.

The more specific you are about your content strategy and what you expect it to accomplish, the more successful your content will be. It isn't enough to define success as "more traffic" or "increased sales" when directing your Marketing AI's content marketing distribution. You need defined audience segments, quantifiable metrics, and measurable results. Marketing automation is one way to keep everything on track; by letting you discover more about what your audience wants, reaching it with triggered messages, and engaging it with targeted content.

Customer Profiling — Buyer Personas

In chapters 3 and 4 (the discovery process) you learned who your customers were and developed buyer personas modeled on them. Using that insight to create buyer personas is an essential ingredient for creating relevant, effective content. Creating buyer personas helps you to research and write about the topics that attract and resonate with your buyers. Buyer personas combine demographic job details with the solutions to challenges your audience frequently encounter and that channels buyers use and trust to find information about the solutions they need. Buyer personas also help you to identify topics and writing styles that will be most effective with your audience. For example, a professional, scientific, and educational style would appeal to doctors, while a conversational, consultative style would be more appropriate when writing content that is targeted at a CEO.

Types of Content — Worth More than a Thousand Words

We've emphasized throughout this book why it's vital to deliver the right information at the right time, and here — in content marketing — is where it matters most. Give prospects too much information early in their buyer's journey, and they aren't ready to make use of it. Deliver too little content in the middle and end of the funnel, and you lose their interest. Your Marketing AI plays a critical role in establishing the right nurture track for your leads, then in catering to them with the right information for their stage of the buying journey.

Content for the Top of the Marketing Funnel

At this stage, your potential customers *sense* that they have a problem and are still fact-finding. They have enough information to recognize your brand, but they haven't yet committed to or signed up for more content from you. Therefore, your content creation team's focus here is to offer information that encourages deeper exploration, answering the "who" and "what" questions on the Lead Lifecycle diagram. You don't want to flood them with jargon-laden articles, webinars, or in-depth case studies at this point, because you haven't established that they're ready to accept these from you. Your MAI's lead-scoring system gives interactions with this content a lower priority than contextual cues from leads that explore deeper content.

Top-of-funnel content includes:

- Articles
- Short-form social media blasts

- SEO articles
- Overview blog posts
- Infographics
- Brief YouTube videos
- Promotions

Establishing Authority in the Middle of the Marketing Funnel

As they move deeper into your Marketing AI's nurture program, your leads *know* that they have a problem, and have some idea how your offer solves it. They've given you enough of their data to establish a dialogue, but they're still deciding whether or not to choose you. Your content's role here is building your authority by educating your prospects. They want proof that you're a leader in your industry, so content at this phase is usually longer and more specific than the information designed for newer leads. They want their "when," "where," and "how" questions answered in greater detail.

Note that some content types appear in more than one portion of the funnel. Some content channels can effectively carry useful information for leads at every level of your sales funnel, and with your Marketing AI, you can tailor delivery of that content to each customer using JavaScript tokens.

Middle-of-funnel content includes:

- E-books and print books
- White papers
- Calculators and self-tests
- In-depth blog posts and articles
- Subscription-based, topic-specific newsletters
- Promotions

Approaching the End of the Funnel with In-Depth Content

At the later stages of their trip through your sales funnel, your prospective customers need to know details, and they need to know why you're their best choice. You're still establishing your authority, but now you're doing so with an audience that has amassed some intellectual authority, too. They want to know the answers to questions that an expert is likely to give them, and you must be that expert to win their business. Some of them are past customers who already know your bona fides and now need the details on a different set of purchases. These clients already want to choose you or they wouldn't be here. At this point, your content marketing strategy should be to validate that choice.

Bottom-of-funnel content includes:

- Deep-dive webinars
- Case studies
- Testimonial videos
- Pricing promotions
- Promotions

It's worth noting that all phases of the buyer's journey involve promotions. There's a reason we included them on the Lead Lifecycle diagram and in this chapter: Promotions are always important catalysts for action. The type of promotion you use is still heavily dependent on where your lead is in the funnel, so contextual cues are as important here as ever. Introductory offers have the most appeal at the top of the funnel, while loyalty programs most effectively reach the prospects near the base of your sales funnel. Product promotions should be rotated with no more than one product promo for each three pieces of content sent.

Multipurpose Content

Content for content's sake isn't useful to you or your readers — it's just more noise. Everything you produce should serve a purpose, and with a Marketing AI managing your content stream, most of it serves multiple goals at once. To your audience, content exists to educate them, and that's important, too. It's part of the larger picture, though, and while it's the fundamental point of your content, that's just the beginning of what content does for you in an AI-assisted marketing strategy.

Content as an Information-Gathering Tool

Many visitors interact with your website anonymously. These visitors have not yet identified themselves with their email address, so your contact strategies are limited. A gating strategy offers a valuable asset as an inducement to the visitor to provide their contact information by placing a form in front of your most valuable content. It typically asks for first and last name, email address, phone number, job title, and company name, but those initial pieces of valuable data can lead to much more. Progressive profile gating asks for a little more information each time as leads move through content gates, until your Marketing AI builds a complex, detailed view of that lead by the MQL stage.

Content as a Motive Force

Your content isn't just informational. It also propels leads through the Lead Lifecycle, taking them from the early, basic "who" and "what" questions through the "how" and "where" of the middle portion of the funnel and on to the "why" as they approach sales readiness. Your initial content might be an SEO article or retweeted link to a blog post that introduces a prospect into your sales funnel. Middle-of-funnel content is designed to lead readers deeper and establish your bona fides as a thought leader. At the bottom of your funnel, it prepares leads for the transition to sales, ensuring that the hand-off is as smooth as possible. Your Marketing AI categorizes content into streams and delivers the right message to the right audience at the right stage of the Lead Lifecycle.

Content as a Quality Indicator

Your content doesn't just teach leads about the subject you're discussing; it also teaches them about you. When it's well crafted, knowledgeable, and purposeful, it sends a strong signal of quality. If it's poorly written or doesn't seem relevant, the message isn't as positive.

Content Marketing versus Native Advertising

One concept that's closely linked to content is native advertising, but these two marketing tools are not the same. Although they both involve creating and distributing content, they serve different purposes. It's important to draw this distinction between content and advertising, because conflating them can cause you to create content that doesn't establish your authority and advertising that fails to persuade. While both are designed to guide leads' progress through the Lead Lifecycle, your goals for content marketing are different from those for your advertising efforts. Let's take a closer look at how native advertising and content marketing differ, so that your MAI can effectively manage both asset types.

Content marketing is strategic; native advertising is tactical. With content marketing, you and your content team provide your audience with a steady stream of relevant, useful information that builds your authority over time. Native advertising is meant to guide specific buying decisions during specific campaigns and has a shorter half-life. Content marketing attracts customers to your websites, landing pages, and social media channels, but native advertising is usually placed on a pre-existing platform, such as an online magazine or an article-marketing site.

To put it another way, you own and distribute your content marketing assets, and you buy space for your native advertising. If assets appear on channels you control, including your blog, company website, email, and newsletters, they fall under the aegis of content marketing. If you pay to distribute it elsewhere, including payment via revenue sharing, it's advertising.

SEO and Content Marketing

SEO is a huge part of digital marketing, and you'll encounter it again in Chapter 12. But it's so important to your overall content strategy that we'll touch on it here, as well. SEO ensures that people can find your content. Without it, you could be publishing work that revolutionizes your industry, but no one will ever know. As with native advertising, SEO is a complementary part of the complex whole that is content marketing. With it, you broaden the top of your sales funnel considerably and give prospective customers plenty of answers to their "who" and "what" questions.

The key to using SEO well is to make it part of a strategic plan, not a temporary tactic. All it takes is one wave of algorithm changes from Google to erase all the traffic gains from a short-term SEO scheme that relies on thin content, keyword stuffing, and content-mill articles. Even when these tactics work for a short time, which they rarely do as those algorithms have gotten more sophisticated, they don't lead to lasting traffic or higher revenue.

A well-founded SEO strategy rests on custom-written content that uses keywords naturally, has intrinsic value to readers, and incorporates links intelligently. In fact, it's sometimes hard to separate well-crafted SEO content from any other form of content marketing. Good content becomes more valuable as you supply more of it, and SEO content counts toward that sum. Integrating SEO into your overall content marketing is a sound long-term strategy, as well as a good short-term investment. Search engines love synergy, and by combining short but informative SEO pieces with longer, in-depth content, your Marketing AI gives them what they want while delivering your prospects the information they need at each stage in the Lead Lifecycle.

Building Authority with Content Marketing

Everything you publish contributes to your audience's perception of you. Ideally, that perception is one of knowledgeable, authoritative expertise. SEO content gives your top-of-funnel traffic a boost, but those gains will be temporary if your new visitors don't get what they expect to find from the rest of your content. Marketers and business owners who invest heavily in SEO alone, without supplying sufficient information to welcome curious prospects to dig deeper, will lose their audiences' interest exactly when they should be encouraging it toward the middle and end of the sales funnel.

Where are your areas of expertise? That knowledge has tremendous value to your blog's readers, and when you and your content creation team blog about it, you encourage visitors to share that knowledge with new readers. The more details you offer, the more authority your words have and the deeper into the sales funnel your content propels your prospects. There are no shortcuts here: Authority takes time and effort to build. The good news is that the process never stops; every blog post you publish, every newsletter you send and every white paper you share lends weight to your words.

The ability of your Marketing AI to deliver the right content at the right time also helps establish your brand authority. If the waiter at your favorite restaurant is able to anticipate your needs, filling your glass precisely when it needs to be filled and telling you every detail of the chef's most enticing special, you feel as though you're in good hands. Clearly, a knowledgeable professional is taking care of you. Your MAI accomplishes the same authority for your brand by serving appropriate, relevant content while it's hot. Marketing automation ensures that you prove not only your industry knowledge, but also your knowledge about your customers' needs. That sends a powerful signal about your brand.

Creating Compelling B2B Content

All the careful content marketing in the world won't help your company if your content's subject matter is dull. Too often, B2B companies assume that because their products are utilitarian, the content the company presents can't be creative, colorful, and clear. These subjects may take a little extra thought on your content-creation team's part to make them sing, but think of H. L. Mencken's assertion: "There are no dull subjects. There are only dull writers." You have an affinity for the subject, you can show your visitors more about the people behind your products, and can offer a fresh look at familiar topics.

Mencken, who never wrote a dull line in his life, would have been appalled at some of the noise many sites publish in the mistaken belief that quantity matters more than quality. If inexpert writers can make an all-inclusive Caribbean vacation sound less exciting than a crowded bus ride across town on a cloudy day, what will they do for a B2B company that sells industrial cleaning supplies? Your writing should have a voice and a personality to it that makes it compelling and resonant to an audience whose first experience with you might be this top-of-the-funnel SEO content. At later stages, the personalized content your Marketing AI chooses to send automatically increases interest when each member of your audience feel it was tailor-made.

Some subjects aren't so much dull as they are perplexing to those outside the industry. A labor-law attorney, for example, has far more knowledge about that specialized legal field than the clients seeking information, but those clients shouldn't need a background in law to find out the five most important things the human resources manager should do to prevent costly litigation. When your content creation team builds content around personas and looks for ways to streamline and clarify challenging subjects, you're rewarded with well-informed, educated prospects whose trust you've earned by giving them valuable information. They've taken a large part of their buyers' journeys with you and are willing to continue if you give them a little expert guidance.

People love a story, and if you can frame information as narrative, they'll follow the tale you and your content creator tell. Let's look at a company that supplies latex gloves to doctors, cooks, and clean-room techs. An article about manufacturing those gloves could be dry, but reframing it with a narrative flow that follows one particular pair of gloves from raw materials and blending to molding and QC communicates the same information in a livelier way. By giving a story a beginning, middle, and end, you immediately increase interest. Thanks to your Marketing AI, you can also customize the message, sending a different story to each of those industries, demonstrating unique value to each audience segment.

At their heart, business transactions are still interpersonal relationships, and any relationship is strengthened when the parties involved know one another a little better. Share something of yourself, your company, and your personnel in your content. Invite your subscribers in to see how the sausage or the software is made. Let them see the people behind the products they buy. Adding the occasional monthly profile of one of your employees to your blog or communicating your excitement about your latest equipment upgrade puts a personal face on your relationship with your prospects. With your MAI, you already know some details about them; your content can turn that knowledge into a two-way street.

Before every election candidates have voter drives to get as many potential supporters registered and headed to the booths as possible. Think of publicizing your content and cross-referencing it via social media channels as your own version of a voter drive. It's a myth that great content will always find an audience without at least a little effort on your part. Especially in B2B sectors, companies have a tendency to silo their content, concentrating on the activities of publishing newsletters and keeping up with social media. Automating these activities so your creative team can put its efforts into content creation gives you more time to focus on the bigger picture.

Your Marketing AI controls distribution and publicity to link social media, SEO, and other content streams together so each acts as a force multiplier for the others. When everything you publish leads back to other branded content, your audience for each channel grows.

Your typical prospects interact with you in multiple ways, especially in today's information-rich climate. They might read a tweet with a link to your blog post, click that link, follow a link in your blog to a landing page, alt-tab to a new window to check out some articles, and possibly download a white paper or two. Only then do they click through the landing page to get to your site. If any of these channels seem out of tune with the others, that discordant note can be enough to interrupt a prospect's flow through your marketing and sales pipeline.

Analyzing the Effectiveness of Your Content Marketing

Content is often difficult for conventional marketing software to quantify. Your return on other investments is measurable, but how do you monitor the impact your latest blog post has had on buying decisions? How do you know the meaning of the behavioral and contextual cues readers give you as they interact with your content? Your MAI can tell you what no other marketing software can, and give you a comprehensive, actionable usage analysis that informs your content marketing strategy. A Marketing AI documents attribution, engagement, views, downloads, and how closely correlated viewing a piece of content is to a prospect's conversion to a customer.

You've learned how to develop buyer personas modeled on your customers. Your content-marketing strategy should speak to each of these customer personas on a personal level — something only a Marketing AI can do. With automation, you take this idea to its logical conclusion and deliver completely customized, one-on-one content. It's as close as you can get to being all things to all prospects, and we'll look at this in greater depth in Chapter 8, which is about personalization.

Takeaways:

1. Your content is your top sales person, so make sure it's educational and distinct.
2. Buyer personas help identify topics and writing styles that will be most effective with your audience.
3. Content should be crafted specifically for top, middle, and bottom of the funnel.

CHAPTER 8

PERSONALIZATION

Since the earliest days of modern data marketing, research has shown that personalized, customized content has a dramatic and positive impact on how that content is perceived. Everything from email open and click rates to time spent on websites increases when content reaches people personally. It makes sense — we all answer to our names, so personalized content makes us pay closer attention. Technology has advanced to the point where you can customize everything you publish for each reader, even on home pages, landing pages, and email.

When personalizing direct mail, email, and other correspondence, it's no longer enough to use your recipient's name in an email subject line or in an envelope window. Hundreds of other mailers are doing that, too. Personalization addresses who a reader is, not just a name. This is where your Marketing AI's brilliance really shows. With it, your mailing list answers myriad questions about your customers as a whole and individually. What title does your prospect have at work? What are her responsibilities at the office? Does your reader have decision-making capabilities, or is this person an end user of your products? Your MAI knows, and it's able to act on that knowledge.

It's also possible to customize and personalize your visitors' web experience on your site. You see it with many of the biggest and most successful B2C companies, but it's equally applicable for B2B. Amazon has built tremendous value into its brand, in part on the strength of its on-site personalization. When customers go to an Amazon page, they're greeted by name, see selections of titles geared to their prior choices, and get customized pages based on their preferences. Notice how every Amazon page also features an "other customers who bought this item liked" section? That's an example of how personalization leads directly to a more customized experience for your visitors and a more effective website for you.

Advances in marketing automation put that technology within the reach of all businesses. You no longer have to be an Amazon or a Microsoft to market directly, knowledgeably, and personally to your prospects.

Personalized content generates the initial interest necessary to turn casual visitors into prospects and prospects into customers. With personalization you're able to make a buyer's journey feel like a road you travel together. It also lets customers navigate those miles along their buying journey more quickly (see Velocity in the Four V's of Big Data section in Chapter 4), because they have all the information they need to make important decisions.

You know that content is key, but by making that content personally relevant, you give it tremendous power. It's ineffectual for one marketer or even a team to have a one-on-one conversation with every prospect, but with your Marketing AI you're able to have those personalized conversations. Behavioral and contextual data are critical to customization, and here you'll discover how your Marketing AI can interact individually with your prospects and customers, giving them meaningful interactions that lead directly to more revenue.

The Fundamentals of Customizing Content

In Chapter 7 we stressed that you can't be relevant until you know your audience and have the appropriate content ready to serve that audience. Learning about your audience personas and what's relevant to them is a big part of the discovery phase of your marketing cycle and what your data enhancement process addresses. Now it's time to fuse that accumulated customer knowledge with your content to speak to each prospect directly via your Marketing AI.

Data is at the core of your marketing efforts, as you learned in Part II. Every bit of data you have from your prospects, leads, and customers gives you another way to deliver a more thoroughly customized experience for them. We all listen more closely when we hear information that speaks to us personally. Ideally, your goal is to make your interactions feel like one-on-one conversations, rather than a single speaker giving a presentation to thousands of anonymous audience members. The more closely you can approximate that one-on-one conversation, the more attentive your audience will be.

Names are the first step to personalization, but they're only the beginning. All your demographic, firmographic, behavioral, and contextual data help you deliver customized content. For example, a CPA firm may reach out to subscribers near milestone birthdays with content pertaining to paying for college or retirement income based on data it has about those prospects. An update to marital status could trigger an email that guides the recipient to content about joint financial planning or asset protection. A prospect that downloads a guide on managing payroll suggests a keen interest in corporate accounting, and triggers a cascade of content and offers geared to business rather than personal finance.

Real-Time Personalization

Real-time personalization (RTP) gives you the ability to target each prospect and customize that lead's user experience. By leveraging the information you have in your database to present a lead with unique and actionable content based on his intent, behavior, firmographics, demographics, and buying potential, you make that content relevant to him. Real-time personalization is all about relevance, but it also addresses timing. It presents the right content at the right time, while you have your prospect's attention and while he's engaged with you.

Your Marketing AI uses your database to segment prospects in real-time based on a myriad of attributes, such as their browsing histories, product interest, industry, title, keyword search, and company size, to interact with them in the digital world, even while they're anonymous. Traditional marketing strategies aren't even able to detect and capture these leads, but with a Marketing AI, they're at the top of your sales funnel.

On average, most of the people coming into your website are anonymous. One of the great aspects of RTP is that it allows you to market to anonymous people while they're on your website, serving up content using stored browsing attributes and inferred data from IP addresses to convert these anonymous visitors into known leads and buying customers. RTP techniques work on any website content management system (CMS) system, using the information you have to serve content matched to your prospects' interests so you can bring them farther through the sales funnel.

Let's take a closer look at how RTP answers the "who," "what," "where," "how," "when," and "why" questions of the various stages of the Lead Lifecycle to engage your leads at every phase.

Who: Speaking to Your Target Audience with RTP

Start by identifying whether the "who" you want to target in real-time is an individual or an entire organization. The "who" can even be anonymous, because your Marketing AI has placed cookies on the prospects' browsers and followed them through your website to discover their interests. In addition to communicating directly to an individual, you can also target an entire organization on an account level. This account-based marketing strategy is very effective, because it predetermines the sales potential and fit that prospective companies have with your company. RTP is very good at serving up relevant content on your website, mobile, digital, and social channels to these target companies. RTP is also excellent for retargeting. It can detect in real-time that someone is coming from a particular company's IP address — even if that lead is anonymous — and serve up the right message to the right person at the right time, increasing click-through rates.

The home and landing pages of your website can also be updated in real-time to serve up relevant graphics, copy, and offers based on known demographics or behaviors, such as what visitors searched on before. Real-time personalization therefore lets you address who your audience is even before you know every detail of their customer profiles.

What: Optimizing Your Content

Your Marketing AI uses RTP effectively through autodiscovery, which allows it to map all your content and learn what content is being read by which prospect. Using that information, it can adapt, improve, and fine-tune its predictions of who else should be interested in the content you provide. It can then serve up the content that most resonates with each prospect based on that lead's profile. Through RTP, your Marketing AI gives you a ready-made solution to nurture prospects effectively and propel them through the sales funnel without the need to involve your IT department.

Using RTP and machine learning also yields more useful and predictive analytics. Identifying which demographic is responding to what content and analyzing how that content results in conversions gives your Marketing AI the power to act on this knowledge in real-time, resulting in an immediate, positive impact. To swing the needle on your ROI, you need to know more than how many dollars you're getting from each campaign: You need to understand how many leads you're converting and what the most effective content path is to convert each lead to a new customer.

Where, When and How: Maximizing Marketing Channels' Impact

You can use RTP in virtually every marketing channel, including email, websites, landing pages, retargeting, SEO, PPC, social channels, and mobile apps. You can even use it with analog channels like direct mail, print, and trade shows.

Main website pages can be updated in real-time to serve up graphics and offers of products and services based on search terms or products viewed on previous visits. Data from retargeting, social, and mobile apps can be used to convert, cross- and upsell, and to redisplay information to customers and prospects, moving them through the Lead Lifecycle at a faster rate. Personal URLs, bar codes, and QR codes can be used to take prospects to a personalized website.

In Chapter 5 you learned which content to serve at each stage of the Lead Lifecycle. With RTP you gain the ability to optimize nurture campaigns by tailoring the appropriate content to the specific Lead Lifecycle. When you're able to determine the content and calls to action that are converting best and deliver that content to the target segment, your conversion rates and ROI will soar.

Companies that use RTP show up to a threefold improvement in engagement and increase content downloads by up to 500 percent. As content downloads are a strong indicator of sales readiness, that's vital.

Why: Convincing Leads to Choose You

Think about how much money and effort you spend to get your prospects' attention. When targeted content appears for them in real-time, you're satisfying their quest for solutions when they need it most and displaying your thought leadership. They're already attentive and engaged at this point, so they need content that gives them a reason to become your customer. Real-time personalization does that by demonstrating your attentiveness to their needs.

Here's a list of common demographic fields used to personalize your messages:

Code	Demographic Field
D1	City
D2	Company revenue
D3	Company-specific demographics to use
D4	Competitor
D5	Designations/Certifications
D6	Fiscal year end
D7	Honors and awards received
D8	Industry (SIC)
D9	Language (English, Spanish, French, etc.)
D10	Number of employees
D11	Organizational structure (partnership, corporation)
D12	Personal interests
D13	Purchased - Last 12 Months
D14	Rankings/Stock Indexes: Fortune 500/Inc.
D15	Role
D16	State
D17	Title
D18	Prospect company's website URL
D19	Year founded
D20	Years at current position
D21	Zip

This list defines behavioral fields used to deliver customized content:

Code	Behavioral (Interests clicked or read)
B1	Articles
B2	Blog posts
B3	Books/eBooks
B4	Brochures
B5	Case studies
B6	Emails
B7	Online demo
B8	Product data sheets
B9	Web pages

This list of channels indicates where you can serve your personalized content:

Code	Marketing Channels Used (Preference)
C1	Affiliations - groups and associations
C2	Community
C3	Lead Source
C4	Webinars/webcasts/live streamed events
C5	Podcast
C6	PPC
C7	Preference RSS/XML feeds
C8	Preferred Lead Channel
C9	Public recommendations
C10	SEO
C11	Social media sharing
C12	Social Media Used (FB, Twitter, LinkedIn)
C13	Social network connections
C14	Tradeshow/Roadshow/Seminar
C15	Videos
C16	Webcasts
C17	Website

Preference: The "P" in Personalization

Another key area for customization comes from email-preference pages. Used in email marketing and website design, preference pages allow users to define their own experiences with you, but they also serve as vital sources of information. Preference centers let your customers tell you precisely what they want to hear from you and when. Your MAI tracks and automates this information to make preference updates a hands-off event. When you know what your customers tell you they want to see, you're able to deliver more of what they want. Combined with the fine-grained market segmentation that's possible with your Marketing AI, a preference center is a powerful customization tool.

Preferences are also customer-friendly. They give your visitors and email recipients the power to tailor their own experience, and everyone appreciates having control over their information streams. Frequency and volume are the two major reasons why users unsubscribe from an email list. By letting them select rates they find comfortable and add topics of interest to customize their user experience, you retain subscribers who want to continue a dialogue with you but also want some input on the type of content and the frequency at which it arrives.

In Chapter 9 you'll see how Marketing AI takes personalization to the next level in one of the most flexible and powerful content delivery channels at your disposal: email.

Takeaways:

1. Every communication should feel as if it's one-to-one.
2. Personalization is more than just addressing your audience by first name; it's a deeper understanding of who it is.
3. RTP answers the essential who, what, where, how, when, and why questions.

PART IV

CHANNELS: OMNI-CHANNEL DISTRIBUTION

CHAPTER 9

ELEMENTS OF EMAIL MARKETING

N
o other marketing channel offers better value, wider reach, or more customization options than email marketing. Every phase of the marketing cycle depends on email and everything in this book relates to email marketing. Social media may have more buzz and direct mail has a longer history, but email is the most consistently productive marketing channel for most businesses, especially those in B2B sectors.

For customer acquisition, email is unparalleled in scope. As a retention tool, it keeps you connected to your prospects and customers. It builds brand recognition, fosters communication, puts you foremost in your prospects' minds and gives you the opportunity to learn more about your audience so your next campaign becomes even more successful. Through win-back programs, real-time personalization, and triggered events, email can even recover customers you thought were lost. But despite these impressive capabilities, many companies still see email marketing as an adjunct to their main advertising and marketing goals when it should be the cornerstone of their efforts. By granting email marketing the importance it deserves, you automatically gain a major advantage over competitors that haven't yet learned this lesson.

An astronomical 850 billion business emails went out to leads, prospects, and customers in 2015. To be noticed in a crowd that large, you need an attention-getting call to action and better designed, more personalized, and more relevant content.

The Nuts and Bolts of Email

When writing personal email or one-on-one business correspondence, you typically click a button and start typing. Email marketing on a wide scale, however, isn't something you can do from your Outlook Express or Gmail dashboard. Sending professional marketing messages starts with gaining insight into how email works and why you can't simply dash off a quick note and forward it to a few thousand of your best prospects.

Marketing emails typically go out through a third-party email service provider (ESP). One reason is convenience, but the crucial reason has to do with your Internet service provider (ISP). All the major ISPs have controls on volumes of mail that can be sent. The volume constraint is set by your historical send-mail rates, which is monitored daily. If you suddenly send 100,000 emails out of a company's email account that has historically sent 1,000 emails a day, your ISP will notice. ESPs have no such restrictions, and so allow you to reach a wider audience. Using an email hosting service that sequentially sends millions of emails a day, from multiple dedicated–IP addresses, avoids these problems and results in improved email delivery. When you set up your account with an ESP, you set the name that appears in the "from" line, which is vital for branding and establishing recognition. As you'll learn in our section on testing, the "from" name is as important as any other element of a well-crafted email.

Email Types That Define Your Marketing Strategy

Marketing automation is vastly more powerful than conventional ESP tools because it elevates your email marketing efforts from simple logistics to a broader top-down view. With it, you develop a strategic approach toward email marketing that produces consistent results. Each email you send should serve a larger strategic purpose. Following is a list of five email types and how to deploy them.

1. **Autoresponder emails:** These emails go out in response to actions a recipient has taken. They're generally simple but they're fundamental to marketing automation because they come at critical points along a buyer's journey through your marketing pipeline.

These emails have high engagement rates because they only go out when a lead takes action, such as filling out a newsletter subscription form or entering information onto a form to download a white paper. They typically contain a URL to a download or confirmation page, and that URL is your marketing automation system's cue to track engagement.

2. **Identifiers:** Even with behavioral and contextual data, it's sometimes necessary for your MAI to work a little harder to assess exactly where a lead is in the sales funnel. Identifier emails help pinpoint their location so your marketing automation system can deliver custom content to them. With these emails you offer a variety of options that let customers sort themselves according to sales readiness. For example, an email might have links labeled with two possibilities: "Subscribe Now" or "Learn More." Each tells your marketing team exactly where this recipient is. When including multiple possibilities, keep emails short and direct.

3. **Content-rich emails:** Content marketing is as powerful a tool in email as it is on your blog and social-media channels. Content emails typically contain a compelling teaser of the actual content; the meat of the information is at a link the recipient clicks through to reach. Give your email recipients the content they need to make buying decisions, and you're doing much of their work for them.

4. **Invitations:** As email recipients narrow their focus to you and your product line, encourage that interest with invitations to download in-depth information and or participate in webinars. Invitation emails appeal to customers who are farther along the sales funnel and are ready to learn more about the details of what you have to offer them. These emails excel at driving attendance to an event — and attendance is highly correlated with sales.

5. **Sales-nurturing emails:** One of marketing automation's greatest strengths is its ability to support nurture campaigns for leads at every step of the sales qualification process. B2B sales cycles tend to be longer than in B2C sectors, so effective lead nurturing, even late in the sales cycle, is critical to keeping potential customers interested and moving ahead. Highly specific and goal-oriented,

sales nurturing emails are brief messages from a seller to alert a customer (who's nearing the end of the sales funnel) to information that could help make a buying decision easier. This email is not a direct ad for your product, but a personalized message offering more information or following up on a recent conversation. Typically, nurture campaigns support the top, middle, and bottom stages of the Lead Lifecycle with their own distinct content streams.

Standard HTML, Plain Text, and Responsive Email Design

You may want your email to be colorful, eye-catching, and impossible to ignore, but not every recipient is using a device that can display an email as you designed it. Some office computers still use CRT monitors or have firewalls that don't permit video or some HTML content to reach end users. Other readers have mobile devices that compress a detailed image on a wide-screen desktop monitor into an indecipherable, postage stamp–size blur on the small screen. You have three options for your email design: conventional HTML, responsive email, or plain text.

When you write HTML email, it does all the things your website can do, including embed video, display images, and create buttons. By going beyond plain text and adding these extras, HTML email gives you the same freedom and creative power you have on your website. Like a website, HTML email needs to be designed rather than just written, and that means giving some thought to composition, fonts, and imagery, as well as to the text itself. Writing your own code is one way to get the job done, but for most businesses working with a marketing company that offers HTML email design is a better option.

Your readers have gone mobile, and more than half your audience now reads email from a smartphone, tablet, or other mobile device. They might check email a dozen times a day from their desktop computers, but they check their phones for various pieces of information an average of 150 times a day. Ignoring half your potential audience by creating email that's difficult to read on a smaller screen is a losing proposition. It's a short jump from glancing at your phone for the time to interacting with it to check your email, so responsive design is a must.

Responsive design treats the elements on a website or email as fluid, modular components that rearrange and resize themselves to suit the screen on which they're displayed. Your information automatically customizes itself to the recipient's device and specifications, instead of staying in a rigid grid. That flexibility allows images and text to display properly on all devices, regardless of screen size. Mobile versions of a responsive email pare away visual clutter and ensure that recipients can see and read all the necessary information. Readability is crucial to response rates, so although responsive email design takes a little more effort to set up initially, it's worth the investment.

In addition, both standard HTML and responsive emails must have a plain-text version for people whose devices don't support images at all or those who simply prefer to cut out all the extras. Email marketing services also provide plain-text versions of your message for those who prefer to get their email that way or who read their email on a device that doesn't support graphics.

The adaptive, fluid design behind responsive email works on current devices, but it also represents an investment in future technology. Email templates that work on current platforms will also work on newly released devices, allowing you to keep your brand consistent through time.

Permissions and Email Marketing

Laws governing email marketing require businesses to follow certain guidelines, such as including a functioning unsubscribe link, listing your organization's physical address, and using accurate subject lines. Marketing best practices treat permissions with great respect. Permission-based marketing lays the groundwork for an ongoing relationship with your prospects.

Implied Permission

Implied permission covers all situations in which you haven't sought express permission from a specific prospect. It includes sending email promotions to current customers on the assumption that they've bought from you in the past and would like to know more about upcoming deals and product launches. When possible, welcome prospects to opt in after having demonstrated your value to them near the top of your sales funnel.

Explicit Permission

When you seek explicit permission, you ask prospects directly if it's all right to contact them. You might do this at a trade show or seminar after talking (in person) with prospective customers, and finishing the conversation with "May I send you more information?" or "May I scan your attendee card and contact you about this?" Explicit permission also includes asking visitors to your website to subscribe to an email newsletter, fill out a form, sign up for notifications, or add their names to your guest book. Offering buyers a button to click to join your email list during the buying process is another form of explicit permission.

Explicit permission extends to list rental services. Recipients on third-party subscriber lists have already given their permission to receive information from other marketing sources, even though they haven't been expressly asked by specific organizations before establishing contact. Many magazine, journal, and newsletter subscription forms include a notification or privacy policy statement that subscriber information may be shared, and users who accept this subscriber agreement also have given their permission to receive relevant marketing messages from list buyers.

You can further segment explicit permissions by your preference-center settings, a tool we discussed in Chapter 8. Preference centers give your audience a line-item veto for correspondence. Trust is vital to the relationship you have with your customers, and letting them choose the kinds of communication they want with you is an important step toward earning that trust. For example, your permission page for email notifications might include opt-ins for email notification of promotions, newsletters, new-product launches, webinars, trade show information, and shopping cart reminders.

In chapters 7 and 8, you learned about the importance of quality content and personalization in marketing success. When seeking explicit permission, you're essentially asking your prospects to volunteer to be marketed to. You can convince them to say yes to that by demonstrating value. Content matters, in part because it's your proof that you deserve to be let in the door when you ask via your call to action or on your preference page. Implied permission is a much faster way to build your email database than explicit, which is why many organizations start with an implied strategy then move their more engaged and prime audience to explicit.

Increasing Deliverability

No amount of work you invest into your email marketing matters if your messages are filtered by ISPs. Even legitimate, relevant communications can become undeliverable if ISPs block the sender. Before we move on to learning about creating amazing content in email, let's look at how to make sure that your content gets where it's meant to go.

Unsolicited email is not necessarily unwelcome email. Most recipients would welcome relevant email that has something of value to offer. Email recipients typically take fewer than three seconds to decide what to do with a piece of mail — not much time to make the desired impression. When they see unknown senders, read a subject line that isn't sufficiently compelling, or find the topic irrelevant recipients aren't shy about disposing of the email — and at worst, they may block the sender.

Different ESPs use their own algorithms to filter email. Spotting IP addresses that send out large volumes of irrelevant email are relatively easy to blacklist, but parsing subject lines to filter email requires some fuzzy logic. Some words are more closely associated with irrelevant sellers than others — that doesn't mean these words are forbidden, but they should be used judiciously. Other elements that automated filters and human readers tend to devalue when deciding what to do with email marketing messages include:

- Hyperbolic phrases, such as *once in a lifetime* or *best ever!*
- Exclamation points and extraneous symbols, such as asterisks or underscores in subjects
- Typing in all capital letters
- Multicolor fonts
- Single-image email messages

- High word density
- Poor grammar and spelling
- Large email size
- Attachment(s)

It's best if your company has its own distinct email server with its own unique IP address. If that's not possible, you should periodically check to see whom you're sharing your server with. You can do this by going to an IP reverse-lookup website, such as IP address.com/reverse-IP/, and enter your domain name or IP address of your email server to see a list of domains sharing that server. Make note of their domains and key those into your browser to visit their websites to make sure the neighbors on your server are reputable companies. If you're sharing server space with businesses that lack your good reputation, it may be time for a move. Most commercial filters automatically report IP–source addresses that generate large volumes of irrelevant mail; even a legitimate business could be reported if it uses shared IP addresses. To minimize your risk of losing your audience to ISP blocks, follow these best practices when mailing:

- Introduce yourself to new prospects. An introductory email is a good way to build familiarity and demonstrate relevance.
- Use permissions wisely and adhere to customer preference-center choices.
- Include your opt-out link at the bottom of your page. Some email marketers put it in the subheader, but it's best saved for the bottom of the page, where recipients can easily find it and where it won't occupy space in the most valuable real estate on your email.
- Proofread and check links. A professional-looking email with clean images and functioning links is far more likely to be received well. If your email doesn't look as though you invested much time or thought in it, why should your readers give it any attention?
- Use a trigger to automatically send a confirmation email when readers opt in or subscribe. By sending them a confirmation, you

are increasing the chance of having future emails opened and verifying that the email address is valid.

- Introduce yourself again if it's been a while since you contacted your email list members or if you're re-targeting them after a hiatus. Someone who signed up for a special offer two years ago won't remember being on that list today and may perceive a newsletter that suddenly appears as unsolicited, even though you once received explicit permission to mail.

Mailing Lists and Prospecting

After gaining some insight into how email comes together, your next consideration is to figure out where all that knowledge will go. How do you get email marketing lists? Your two best options are to build your own list or rent one from a list management firm. The two possibilities aren't mutually exclusive, either; you can have your own house list while renting access to others. Depending on your permissions and original user agreement for your house list, you can even open it for rental yourself, turning the information you've garnered into a valuable commodity.

Building Your Email List

We stressed the importance of list hygiene, in Chapter 3 in particular, and of gathering additional information during the discovery phase and using your list for retargeting. But that work doesn't end with discovery. Each thing you send gives you an ever-increasing wealth of behavioral, contextual, and firmographic data on your prospects. Blog posts that have subscription links; white papers that ask for email addresses for delivery; customer service calls that request email addresses as a routine part of service; social media channels that ask readers to contact you for more information; point-of-sale processes that include an opt-in for your newsletter — all are critical to building a house list.

Incentivize joining your house list with loyalty programs, deals for subscribers, early access for members, and other value propositions. People need a reason to volunteer to be marketed to, so give them those reasons with great content and incentive programs. Your prospects respond best to email they signed up to receive, so make list building and maintenance a priority.

Progressive Profiling

One way Marketing AI streamlines the process of list building is to create forms using progressive profiling. Progressive profiling allows your AI to encourage sign-ups by keeping your forms short and easy to complete, and it's smart enough to skip questions previously answered by your prospect. Each successive time a lead fills out a form, your AI asks new questions that progressively collect new and valuable information about them. By serving up a smart, progressive form, you encourage unknown prospects to become known leads. When you get an email address and go from passive data collection to active marketing, you control the content — and with it, your business's destiny.

Most marketers put too many questions on a form because they think the answers are equally important. They feel a great urgency to gather information, yet the more questions they ask, the less likely they are to get responses. With progressive profiling, you ask only the essential questions with each touch. This iterative profiling process minimizes friction and maximizes conversions from anonymous to known contacts. Instead of overwhelming leads with lengthy forms, your MAI prioritizes data collection to build a customer profile from the bottom up, starting with the most vital information first. Over time, you're able to collect a treasure trove of important firmographics and contextual information about product interests so that you can serve each prospect more relevant content. Since you ask the most important questions on the initial form and gather increasingly finer detail on each successive form, progressive profiling allows you to collect the right amount of information at the right time.

Segmentation

You first encountered segmentation in Chapter 3 (data governance), but it's just as important for defining mailing lists and separating email streams into lead nurture programs for top-, middle-, and bottom-of-funnel leads. Segmentation also helps when building your house list. Your long-term customers will respond positively to loyalty programs while new prospects get more from an email focused on their job function or industry. Here's where knowing where your leads are in the sales funnel matters most. Specificity and customization hold greater appeal than generic email blasts, so take the time to address your list members individually. Make it feel like a one-on-one experience, and they'll respond. It starts with your initial email so don't neglect these cornerstones of your list-building efforts.

List Rentals to Expand Your Audience

Renting a list gives you a short cut, plus the most direct access to a large, preselected audience of prospects. In Chapter 4 we talked about the importance of defining your customer profile and mapping it against other profiles to find the closest matches. Here's where that information becomes pivotal to using list rental as part of your email marketing strategy. By understanding your list rental options, you can identify the lists that best serve your marketing needs, select the right segments within those lists, and deliver relevant, customized offers to list members.

When list renting you need to know the kind of list it is and how it relates to your customer profiles. For example, a compiled list of email addresses from a specific geographical area may be ideal for a restaurant that serves lunch specials to a local crowd. For one that wants to reach sales professionals who have corporate gift–purchasing authority, a response list from a database containing magazine subscribers, members of a professional association, or buyers from an e-commerce company would be the better choice.

Other prospecting sources include:

- **Referrals:** Let your customers help you find new leads. Reviews are important to B2C marketing, but good word-of-mouth referrals are vital to B2B sectors. Asking for referrals is straightforward and often produces good results. Even if they have no pressing need for your product, they may know someone who does. Don't be shy about asking them for referrals or suggesting they forward your email messages to people they feel might want to receive them, too; you stand to lose nothing and there is much to gain by asking your prospects to suggest other prospects. Formal referral programs that reward customers for bringing new subscribers to you may also be a good route to house-list building.

- **Business directories:** Your local Chamber of Commerce or other business directories can be valuable sources for prospects. Directories organized by industry have already done part of your work for you by segmenting your audience, but don't be afraid to venture out of your comfort zone to find complementary markets.

- **Trade shows, conferences, and webinars:** We discuss trade shows in greater detail in Chapter 14, but they merit a mention here, too. Trade shows add significant value to your house list because they're composed of people who already have a stated interest in what you offer. Sharing information at a trade show or through a webinar sign-up is a form of explicit permission and puts you in touch with a highly motivated audience. If your industry doesn't lend itself to trade shows directly, you might still benefit from them by renting trade show attendee lists.

- **Professional organizations:** From apple growers to zipper manufacturers, almost every trade or industry has a professional group associated with it. Membership lists for these organizations are a rich source of leads. Not only can current members of professional organizations pass your name along to their colleagues, but they can also point the way to similar associations that probably have other members who fit your customer profile.

Create Email Content Using the IOU Principle

Cutting through the noise to make your voice heard by the people who matter most to your business is summed up in one straightforward concept: the IOU principle. IOU is an acronym for generating *interest*, making a compelling *offer*, and creating a sense of *urgency*—the three steps to effective email. The principle is easiest to see in email but you'll see it in other content once you know how to look for it. SEO, blog posts, tweets, and landing pages frequently use it. It's especially useful on short-term and mid-range campaigns with limited time scales, but almost all your content contains some element of the IOU principle. It gets to the heart of what marketing is supposed to do. If your campaign lacks a persuasive offer, your potential customers have no compelling reason to act. Fail to create a sense of urgency, and prospects feel they can afford to wait on your offer, often forgetting about it entirely by the time they move on to the next message. Your marketing strategy must contain these three fundamentals to succeed.

The IOU principle applies to every aspect of your campaign, but it's especially important to the three main parts of your email message: the subject line, the pre-header and the body of the mail. Creating interest, making an offer and building urgency should happen in each of these three areas for maximum effect.

Subject Line

Your subject line is the single biggest influencer of open rates. Without a captivating subject line to grab your audience, recipients won't ever see the stylish graphics and crisp copy on the inside. Here's a subject line that hits all the IOU sweet spots: "Free Webinar — Find Your Next Customer! Only One Day Left"

Use these key words in your subject line to increase your response:

- **"Free"** *Free* remains one of the greatest interest generators you can use in a subject, so it's at the front of the line.
- **"You"** – Read through almost any well-written online content, and you'll probably see plenty of second-person writing. In content marketing, *you* and other forms of personalization are potent talismans for creating interest.
- **"Improve"** – *Improve* has tremendously broad appeal. It resonates deeply with people who have a concern that needs a solution, but it also reaches those who are generally satisfied.
- **"New"** – Novelty is an outstanding motivator and driver of interest. Deliver a new process, product, or service that aims to solve

your customers' most pressing problem, and you instantly have their attention.

- **"Rare"** – Scarcity is another outstanding motivator. Change the word from "day" to "seat" in the subject line example below and it still hits all the IOU sweet spots: "Free Webinar — Find Your Next Customer! Only One *Seat* Left"

Preheader

The preheader is at the top of your email above the body copy and renders directly below the subject line on most mobile devices. It is the textual equivalent of an elevator pitch, a chance to tell your customers in a sentence or two exactly why they should be interested in your offer and feel urgency to take you up on it immediately. It should include a link to a landing page (so readers can take action right away), use concise language, and build that sense of urgency to adhere to IOU best practices.

Body

If the subject line and preheader are your greeting and your elevator pitch, then the body is your email's interview. You've successfully made it into the office and earned the right to a few seconds of your recipient's time, so use it well and stay with the strategy that got you there — interest, offer, urgency.

Building Branding into Email Creative

You've learned that a brand is so much more than a name. It extends to everything you do, including email. Respected brands have authority, consensus, and consistency on their side, making effective branding an immensely valuable way to earn and retain customers. Your email plays a key role in establishing mindshare for your brand, even if your prospect doesn't convert on this campaign. You also have the potential to capture that lead on future campaigns, thanks to a Marketing AI system that has robust re-targeting capabilities.

The more well defined you make your brand, the more your email recipients will instantly recognize you. Effective branding must be consistent, so your email should have a distinctive voice that relates to your company's social media channels, static website, and blog. Your readers can open your email to experience your whole brand — the images, products, text, company philosophy, and personality — even when they feel ambivalent about the specific offer. Get them used to seeing great things from you, and they'll open, save, and forward your emails to become your brand ambassadors.

In Chapter 10 you'll learn how direct mail is thriving through innovations in printing, branding effectiveness, and retargeting power. With less clutter than ever, this tactic reinforces your brand identity and legitimacy.

Takeaways:

1. Email is the most important communication channel because it combines speed, reach, customization, and effectiveness.
2. Third-party email lists represent an extraordinary outlet to expand your reach.
3. I, O, and U are the three most important letters in email.

CHAPTER 10

DIRECT MAIL

According to a 2015 study published by *Target Marketing Magazine*, the highest scoring form of marketing for B2C and B2B marketers is direct mail. Direct mail includes any flat letter, brochure, response form, survey, or package you send to prospects and customers at their postal addresses. As printing and postage costs have risen, some companies have turned away from direct mail in favor of email marketing, SEO/SEM or social media, but we feel strongly that no client should rely on any single channel; an omni-channel marketing strategy is considerably more effective than any single avenue of communication. Your audience consumes content in more ways than one, so you want to be wherever it looks and deliver your content via multiple streams as well.

Direct mail is an excellent way for B2B industries to own a channel their competitors have abandoned in the mistaken belief that it no longer pays a good return on their investment. A Marketing AI makes direct mail worthwhile because it delivers highly relevant information to a carefully selected audience using scrupulously clean data.

Direct mail's total cost is typically the highest of all channels, but when used properly it generates one of your highest returns on investments. Domestic and international direct mail from U.S. businesses accounts for more than $2 trillion annually. Obviously, mail sales are still a major part of the marketing landscape, even as email, web, and social media have become indispensable tools for reaching customers. With the shift of B2B and B2C business to digital channels, the direct mail marketplace is a crucial one for companies that are able to leverage the following six unique direct-mail characteristics:

1. **It's personalized.** As we discussed in Chapter 8, personalization is very important to earning conversions after reading and now direct mail is more customizable than ever. Advances in printing technology let you tailor your mail to your audience, eliciting higher response rates and driving your ROI higher. Personal URLs and QR codes take prospects immediately to a custom site, which your content creation team has prepared for them. They're assigned and tracked within your marketing automation system, allowing you to integrate direct mail and digital channels to an unprecedented degree.

2. **It's lasting.** People respond to correspondence they can hold in their hands, tack on a message board, or give to a colleague. By giving your customers something tactile and lasting to reinforce the message you've sent via email and social media, you lend that message greater weight and legitimacy.

3. **It's versatile.** Use direct mail to blanket a small geographical area, selectively contact your most promising prospects, provide PURLs to select leads according to their audience segment, or solidify your brand identity with your customers.

4. **It's instantly noticeable.** When you send direct mail, you're moving into a marketing arena many competitors no longer venture into, immediately giving your mailings higher visibility. It's hard to hear someone shouting in a crowded room, but in one with fewer people, even a whisper speaks volumes.

5. **It's easy to track.** Direct mail gives you quantifiable results to help you focus your future marketing campaigns. Email does this as well, and with direct mail to back it up, you get a multidimensional view of your entire marketing strategy's effectiveness. Your Marketing AI can then use this wealth of data to improve lead nurturing and gain insight into your audience.

6. **It legitimizes your organization's market position.** By reinforcing your email, SEO, and social media messages with direct mail to

give them brand-building mind share, direct mail creates a more lasting and vivid impression of your brand.

Making the Best Use of Direct Mail

Direct mail inevitably costs more than email and social media, but that doesn't mean it has to break your budget. The United States Postal Service (USPS) has programs to make direct mailing less expensive, and selecting your audience carefully before you mail also defrays costs while ensuring high response rates. One key way to keep costs low is through the excellent data hygiene that marketing automation provides. Nowhere is it more important to work from a clean list than with direct mail, so follow the guidelines in chapters 3 and 4 on data governance and data hygiene to make the most of your direct mail spending.

We recommend optimizing your direct mail marketing by focusing its use to achieve these goals. These aren't the only uses for direct mail, but they're an excellent place to start as you expand your omni-channel marketing via automation.

Retargeting

As a retargeting tool, direct mail illustrates your legitimacy to an audience that has already shown some degree of interest in your offer and allows you to maintain a connection with a wavering prospect or customer. Marketing automation excels at coordinating and delivering retargeting campaigns. For trade show attendees or webinar registrants (see chapters 14 and 15), retargeting via direct mail reinforces the content they've already enjoyed from you. Re-engagement with email recipients who opened their email but didn't respond or customers who filled a shopping cart but haven't yet purchased produces results because this audience is already qualified. Their behavioral and contextual data has assigned them a lead score, and your MAI will place them within the appropriate content stream for direct mail just as it does for email, banner advertising, and other channels. They have selected themselves as expressing some level of interest, and direct mail can be the deciding factor that convinces them to take action.

With a fully integrated omni-channel marketing strategy, your email open and click-through rates inform every aspect of your direct mail retargeting campaign. This process is especially cost-effective with a clean, verified list that has gone through data enhancement via appends to give you more information about the intended recipients.

Building Your Brand

Direct mail gives legitimacy to your other marketing efforts, and it's a crucial part of becoming an established brand in your leads' eyes. Your direct mail should be painted with the same palette as the content on your other marketing channels: Use the same logo, typeface, and imagery throughout to reinforce your brand identity. Automation ensures a uniform look while allowing you to customize content. Like your other marketing channels, your direct mail must remain on message, but because a piece of paper gives you more room to expand, you have more space for branding elements. An eye-catching logo or a sleek print brochure makes a lasting impact.

You have additional options for brand building with direct mail because it's more permanent than an email or tweet. A calendar or note pad puts your company's name and logo on recipients' desks where they can see them every day. Familiarity is essential to branding and to developing a rapport with your customers, so anything that fosters it is a worthy investment.

Sending Items

Take full advantage of the tactile nature of direct mail by sending 3-D items. To your recipients, that unopened envelope with something inside it is like a wrapped present. Few people would throw a wrapped gift away without looking inside, and your leads treat items in mail the same way. People find thick envelopes and mailers almost irresistible to open, and adding something as modest as a ballpoint pen to your direct mail increases open rates by as much as 60 percent. For all the benefits email and online marketing offer, they lack the curiosity produced by an envelope with something more than paper inside it.

Anything that adds substance to your direct mail also adds weight, so it's critical to work from a clean list and send to the most receptive members of your audience. Your MAI's lead-scoring capability pinpoints the most receptive prospects and customers, and then places them within the right nurture-campaign flow to carry them through your sales funnel. Frequent buyers, long-time customers, and prospects that have reached out to you for more information via email, phone, or online are good bets for sending items to.

Occupying an Underused Market Space
Companies that send mail have invested more time and capital in their marketing campaigns and must comply with federal regulations governing mail. Email marketing offers a cost-effective alternative to large-scale mailing. Together, those factors limit the number of businesses that use direct mail, opening the door for companies that do use it selectively. Because you're approaching your audience from an unexpected — and largely uncontested — direction, your audience tends to pay closer attention to your direct mail message.

Customizing and Integrating Communications
PURLs turn a single piece of direct mail into an entire library of custom content for recipients. With them, you can invite leads to a landing page, welcome them to a webinar or seminar, and give them access to your most valuable content while providing a personalized experience during every step of their buying journey. Bar codes and QR codes integrate direct mail with online components of your omni-channel marketing strategy, such as Salesforce, Microsoft Dynamics, and other digital tools, so you can create a seamless and uniquely attractive environment through which your prospects move.

Large-Scale Mailing or Selective Mailing?
You can be highly selective about who receives your direct mail with audience segmentation, and your Marketing AI can focus on leads with

an unrivaled degree of granularity. But in some cases saturation mailing can also be a useful tool. For highly localized businesses, for example, sending a postcard with a coupon or special offer to every household or business within a certain ZIP+4 code may produce outstanding results. E-commerce businesses, B2B companies, and organizations that draw from a regional or national audience should mail selectively to qualified or segmented audiences.

The USPS uses the National Change of Address system, or NCOA-Link*, to get mail to the right recipients. Marketers can access NCOA-Link data to enhance deliverability of their brochures, postcards, and other mailers. If you plan to use large-scale mailing, getting accurate information from the NCOA system is a must. With more than 160 million names and addresses, the NCOA system lets you correspond with valued customers and open communications with new leads. Marketing automation takes care of NCOA-Link synchronization for you.

For flat mail within a limited size range, the USPS also offers an Every Door Direct Mail (EDDM) option. EDDM allows SMBs to buy by carrier route, but it's restricted to flat, letter-size mailings. Traditional saturation mailing lets you send postcards, brochures, and envelopes with items, and its cost is often comparable to EDDM. Investigate the possibilities with your marketing team before you choose your direct mail channel.

One of the best options for prospecting to non-customers through direct mail is by using a response-generated direct mail list. These types of lists generate a higher response rate because the people on the list have a proven history of responding by mail. Another thing to consider is specific-language literacy; the respondents who don't read the language the direct mail is written in self-select by removing themselves from your Lead Lifecycle because they are not leads.

Regardless of your offer, a quality response list of magazine subscribers, seminar attendees, catalog buyers or association members will always outperform other types of audience compilations. Since you are making

---

* NCOA-Link processing is provided by a non-exclusive licensee of the United States Postal Service. The following trademarks are owned by the United States Postal Service: ZIP, ZIP Code, ZIP+4, CASS, NCOA-Link, LACS-Link, USPS, U.S. Postal Service, United States Postal Service, United States Post Office.

a substantial investment, the list cost is the least of your expenses but has the largest impact on your overall results.

Advances in Direct Mail Technology

Direct mail has been around for almost as long as we've had postal service. Catalog and mail order sales are still viable and advances in direct mail have updated this venerable marketing channel for the 21st century.

Variable Data Printing

Personalization increases open rates for email and its impact is even more dramatic for direct mail. With variable data printing (VDP), you're able to customize mailings to a far greater degree by including recipients' names, company logos, or other personalized details as part of the imagery, not just within the text of your mail. For example, a technical school offering courses in medical technology might feature an image of a lab coat with your target company's logo on the chest. Although it costs a bit more than standard printing, VDP is an immensely powerful tool for customization and works especially well for small, highly qualified audiences.

QR Codes

Integrate your direct mail marketing with your online presence by adding quick response (QR) codes to your mailed materials. Like bar codes, QR codes occupy little space on your print piece but provide a link from your offline marketing to your online presence. A QR code can direct your audience to a custom landing page or to your website home page. Users can scan a QR code on your brochure or postcard with their phones, then visit your site directly using the code instead of typing in additional information. You may not be able to fit all the information you'd like to share on a small postcard or business card in your direct mail, but with a QR code you can lead recipients to where they can find the information. For technology-oriented industries or brands that prioritize convenience, QR codes also act as a signal of forward thinking. Possible uses for QR codes in direct mail include links to:

- Spec sheets
- Contact information
- Special offers
- Event details
- Contest rules
- Coupons and discounts
- Social media channels
- Videos and podcasts

Direct mail puts you in touch with your audience in a tangible way. In Chapter 11, you'll learn how to enhance that lasting connection by letting your prospects and customers hear your voice through telemarketing.

Takeaways:

1. Direct mail reinforces your organization's legitimacy.
2. Innovative printing technology has rejuvenated the direct mail space.
3. Direct mail is most cost-effective when used for retargeting.

CHAPTER 11

TELEMARKETING

Telemarketing has earned a glamorous new place in modern marketing automation. As a tool to keep leads from becoming losses and for discovering what else you need to deliver to solve a promising lead's problem, it's one of the most effective instruments at your Marketing AI's disposal. The key to using it intelligently is timing, which your AI's Lead Lifecycle automatically controls for you. Of all marketing channels, telemarketing is the one most businesses continually overlook, often because they're uncertain how to qualify their audience for calls without a marketing automation system to score them. That's good news for companies that are unafraid to embrace one of the most effective and least crowded ways to continue conversions at one of the most important points of the Lead Lifecycle.

The ideal time to use telemarketing is at the sales readiness stage of the buyer's journey. At that point your leads have been fully qualified by marketing but haven't yet been accepted by your sales team. This part of the Lead Lifecycle is one of the most critical: It's where your marketing team hands leads off to the sales team, and it's where leads that don't receive appropriate nurturing slip through the cracks.

Before sending the lead to your sales team, many companies use an intermediary step to verify the lead score and qualify the lead's need, authority, budget, and buying priority. Typically, this process involves a quick call by a telemarketing team to validate the lead and to schedule a call with your sales team. During this needs-and-authority assessment, your telemarketing team also contributes to the user experience and verifies a lead's sales readiness. This information then goes back into the Marketing AI to be synched with your CRM system to ensure a seamless transition from marketing to sales.

A study by HubSpot cites the following two statistics to illustrate the profound effect a great telemarketing team can have on the success of your business:

- The first five minutes of response time are critical to higher contact-and-qualification rates. If leads are responded to in fewer than five minutes, the odds of contacting them are 100 times higher than they would be from waiting 30 minutes.
- The recommended number of follow-up attempts is between six and nine calls, depending on the lead type. By making six to nine attempts, you get 90 percent or more of the total value out of the lead.

Data Discovery and Governance for Telemarketing

Data hygiene is at the heart of an effective telemarketing campaign. How do you clean and maintain data across multiple channels? Telemarketing now offers answers. A Marketing AI appends accurate phone numbers to existing data, locates bad area codes, eliminates extra digits, and finds transposed digits to keep all your records up to date; a single phone call provides direct verification of that data. Although your house list is always a valuable resource, working with high quality, specifically targeted, B2B-source lists opens new markets for telesales. Segmented lists that focus on a particular industry or use files from professional organizations and subscriber lists are better values than compiled lists for telemarketing.

After direct mail, no marketing channel relies on good data housekeeping as much as telemarketing. You can achieve impressive ROI numbers when you reach a receptive audience, but if your telemarketing records are clogged with invalid phone numbers, you're wasting your efforts and your telemarketing team's precious energy. Chapters

3 and 4 underscore how important data governance is for your marketing efforts; telemarketing also enhances the discovery process. As callers contact your leads, they can verify information directly for more up-to-date, accurate information in other channels.

Telemarketing enables you to gather data actively. You not only learn if the person you're contacting has buying authority, but also who in the organization does (if you aren't able to reach the contact initially). This gives you far better saturation within a prospect's company. Whether inbound or outbound, B2B calls to companies that have had previous business interactions with you are exempt from most phone registry regulations that apply to calls to personal residences, so having updated business-contact files is especially important for reaching your potential customers where they're most receptive.

Inbound Versus Outbound Telemarketing

Each time a customer or prospect is communicated with via telemarketing, whether inbound or outbound in nature, it introduces a unique opportunity to gain valuable insight about your audience that isn't easily obtainable through any other medium.

Inbound Telemarketing

Often overlooked as a minor part of the sales process instead of a marketing tool in its own right, inbound marketing is far more than simply taking a customer's order. It's an opportunity to add value by cross- or upselling a sale, gather important contact information, amass demographic and contextual data for your MAI, and track sales metrics. Inbound calls give your marketing team insight into customers' pain points and chief concerns even if callers don't become buyers on this call. Call volume, length of time per call, and purpose are vital pieces of information for customer histories and can be tracked within your MAI, then synched with your CRM so your sales team benefits from this knowledge. If you have a dedicated inbound telemarketing staff, don't miss this chance to learn more about your customers and enhance the value of each sale.

Outbound Telemarketing

These calls go from your office or telemarketing center to prospects and customers. Sometimes called cold calling, it's what most people think of when they hear the term telemarketing. It's a misnomer to call effective telemarketing cold calling, though. With customization and appropriately targeted content, your leads are far more likely to give you a warm reception. After prequalifying leads by using segmented call files, gathering key information, and contacting prospects via other marketing channels with your MAI, you aren't going into the interaction cold. AI-assisted outbound telemarketing is an essential part of verifying sales readiness, a checkpoint you can't afford to miss as leads make their buyers' journeys.

Using AI-Assisted Telemarketing Effectively

Telemarketing allows you to reclaim lost leads and guide marketing-qualified leads into the sales portion of your marketing pipeline. Keeping in closer touch with prospects at this critical stage also edges out your competition. As few companies are equipped to use this highly sophisticated, customer-focused form of telemarketing, you take complete ownership of an underutilized channel. Voice communications have a warmth, immediacy, and presence second only to a face to face meeting, so phone communications are also an outstanding relationship-builder, not only for your current leads but for prospects, as well. Your Marketing AI will help you discover this through analysis of their behavioral and contextual data.

Booking Appointments

The fundamental role of a telemarketing call is to urge leads to take the next step, often by making an appointment with sales. People who have shown interest but haven't yet taken the plunge and arranged an interview with one of your sales team members have already traversed most of your Lead Lifecycle; they just need one last touch to trigger a commitment. At this point, leads are highly receptive to telemarketing calls that offer to book on the spot. With a Marketing AI, you're able to pinpoint the right time and place for the call that will give a lead that last bit of momentum to complete the transit of your sales pipeline. Bringing leads to the edge of a buying decision and letting them get lost at the end of the journey wastes a great deal of marketing effort that a single call can prevent.

After setting an appointment with a sales associate, your MAI can also set up email-marketing triggers to follow up with a call after a certain time, upon receipt of a reply, or under other conditions you and your marketing automation specialist set. Follow-up and appointment calls have high conversion rates by themselves, but are even more powerful when used with other marketing channels, and a Marketing AI automatically coordinates these multitouch campaign flows.

Qualifying Leads

Sometimes the best way to qualify a promising lead is to ask directly. Your MAI's lead scoring system identifies the most promising prospects, and your telemarketing team then approaches this receptive audience to pinpoint prospects' needs more precisely, guiding them along the pipeline during a critical phase. A phone call can ascertain the names and positions of company decision-makers, identify where the recipient is along the buying journey, and uncover what additional information you can send to help your lead reach a buying decision.

This lead qualification strategy works best when leads have been preselected from relevant lists that align closely with the offer you're making, which is a process your MAI has streamlined for you. If you're offering construction software, for example, you might choose lists of general contractors, construction company owners, and subscribers to construction-oriented professional journals. When you work with these prequalified and high-scoring leads, your telemarketing calls have less ground to cover to convert.

Verifying Information

In today's job market, turnover is frequent and titles are fluid. Even with a well-maintained file, your marketing may not connect directly with the right person within an organization, but a telephone call instantly updates your MAI's records. In many cases the information in a compiled list takes you only to the first layer of the organization; with telemarketing, you can drill down to reach the people who are in a position to act on your offer. Knowing who these decision-makers are will often lead to other valuable prospects, either by referral or through reconnecting with former contacts that are now with a different organization or in a new department. It's an active way to gain information that your Marketing AI can then correlate with other details in a prospect's record to create a more complete picture of that lead.

Consulting

Giving leads a user experience that draws them farther along the sales pipeline sometimes means *taking* the lead. Telemarketing that plays a consultative role puts you in control of advancing leads' progress while collecting valuable information about what your prospects consider their greatest challenges. As consultants, your telemarketing team also helps recover leads that might otherwise be lost during the transition from marketing to sales by smoothing the path. A marketing-qualified lead's lingering questions are answered, preparing the lead for sales acceptance and the next phase of the buying journey.

Inviting Prospects to Special Offers

Person-to-person communications have special meaning when someone calls to give you good news. An invitation to something special is always good news, and your properly marketing-qualified leads will welcome these contacts. When you have a unique offer to make, telemarketing is a powerful way to get the word out and invite your most promising leads to participate in seminars, webinars, deep discount offers, and beta tests. For offers that have limited space or availability, invitations via phone are especially useful because they place a gateway on access. There's something about giving a verbal commitment that inspires people to follow through. Leads that commit via phone contact have a higher attendance rate for webinars, seminars, and conferences than those that commit solely via email or online sign-ups. If your webinar is too persuasive to miss — and it is if you've followed our suggestions on creating outstanding content — then every attendee counts.

Getting Feedback

Your telemarketing team is human, but the AI assisting it gives you super-human insights into your leads' behavior and the contexts in which they take action — or when they fail to act. Telemarketing prompts specific, detailed feedback that few other channels provide. Making it easy for leads to tell you what they want, which problems they need solved, and when they need a solution improves the user experience and leads to increased satisfaction and lead conversion.

Feedback applies also to customer calls. A sales transaction doesn't stop once a customer has made a purchase. The information you glean from your customers is invaluable for improving your service to them and expanding to new audiences. Storing this data in your MAI and CRM system not only helps you serve these customers better, but also teaches your AI valuable lessons for future use. Telemarketers can conduct full-scale surveys over the phone or gain permission to send a longer survey via email or direct mail.

The Power of Conversation in Omni-channel Marketing

Contacting leads through other means often involves a certain amount of action on their part. With telemarketing, you take the active role. The personal, specific, and instant connection of a phone call, combined with that active participation, makes a conversation on this channel particularly compelling. That's especially important for leads whose activity has dropped and who may be in danger of being lost. Reestablishing a connection with at-risk and newly dormant MQL leads gives you an opening to ask three important questions:

1. How did our solution fail to solve challenges for your business?
2. What made you postpone a solution to your problem?
3. Which solutions are you currently considering for your problem?

Even after a prospect has chosen to go in a different direction, your Marketing AI helps you reclaim some of the cost of nurturing that lead with telemarketing questions that reveal valuable information, such as:

- What drove you to select our competitor as your solution?
- How did our competition meet the objectives you are looking to achieve?
- What are the likely consequences if the solution you chose fails to solve your problem?

Many companies that use telemarketing fail to connect it with their buyers' journeys. Every conversation you have throughout your lead-development and nurturing process builds on previous interactions, effectively moving prospects through the Lead Lifecycle, and nowhere do those conversations have more immediacy than with telemarketing. Integrating your MAS with a CRM system ensures that all communications are thoroughly documented in a customer's file to provide your Marketing AI with a complete history of an account.

If your telemarketing representatives are isolated from where the rest of those conversations take place, they can't effectively carry prospects forward to your desired next step. A Marketing AI integrates telemarketing with other points of contact to create a true omni-channel communications web. In addition to your direct conversations, when using telemarketing within your multitouch strategy you glean significant information from this channel. For example, you can deploy a telemarketing team to phone every prospect that took specific steps that your Marketing AI recognizes as interest signals, yet haven't taken further action.

These prospects have undergone marketing qualification but clearly aren't quite ready for sales acceptance. They have shown an interest but weren't compelled to convert; this is where telemarketing really earns its stripes. Contact these qualified, but potentially lost leads to understand why they have paused along their marketing journey. This critical knowledge can shape your subsequent campaigns by teaching your Marketing AI vital lessons about that lead as well as others, and it might even suggest different strategies or marketing directions. When you're executing these calls, have a predetermined follow-up strategy in place that responds to the feedback you received from your telemarketing efforts.

Your AI classifies telemarketing leads as in progress, recycled, or lost in addition to marking current progress along the Lead Lifecycle. Obviously, if you close the sale over the phone, your welcome flow will initiate. If the prospect is in progress and has reached the MQL stage of your lead pipeline, your marketing automation system's flow might direct an email with a heightened sense of urgency to this lead.

A recycled lead that has been through prior qualification steps and needs additional guidance to make a buying decision might get an email with a kicked up offer, such as an additional discount, free shipping, or an initial month of services for free. For lost leads, the MAI's flow could send an email that restates your offer and focuses more heavily on product and company branding that positively impacts future campaigns and earns referrals. With careful, thoughtful lead nurturing, today's lost lead could be tomorrow's sale.

These follow-up emails should be deployed the same day, if not immediately following, the telemarketing effort. You want to stay foremost in your prospects' minds, and waiting too long can lose you the advantage of an omni-channel campaign. With AI-assisted telemarketing, you won't waste the instant impact of a phone call by waiting too long to follow up.

AI-guided telemarketing is the antithesis of cold calling. It's a way to add warmth and personalization to conversations with leads while guiding them farther along the marketing pipeline from marketing qualification to sales acceptance, sales qualification, and ultimately, to customer conversion.

Telemarketing delivers the human side of your organization and can initiate or transition any lead within the buyer's journey. In Chapter 12, you'll learn the essential role SEO plays in establishing an impactful first impression.

Takeaways:

1. A qualified sales-ready lead deserves your phone call.
2. Telemarketing is an effective way to gain key insights on your audience.
3. Telemarketing generates an unmatched personal, human, specific, and instant connection.

CHAPTER 12

SEO Essentials

Google gives users millions of results, but only eight of them appear on the front page, and more than 80 percent of users never look beyond that first screen. To earn your place on the front page of results, you're engaged in an arms race with your competition — a race many companies don't even realize they're in. Search engine optimization (SEO) is the ultimate weapon in this arms race. It's your most effective option to neutralize the competition for new leads, organic and paid search.

Marketing Sherpa's data states that SEO comes in second only to email marketing as a lead generation tool. It's the ideal complement to email marketing, creating the "pull," or inbound lead generation, which mirrors email's "push" toward outbound lead generation. It's also one of your least costly options, which is why it's one of the top three channels for lead generation among SMBs. But many companies fail to develop a cohesive SEO strategy, despite its proven efficiency as a lead generator and authority builder. The data also states that one in three had 12 or fewer lead generation programs going on annually in 2012 — and that includes monthly SEO content releases. Given that lead generation increases companies' ROI on average by 110 percent, that's a shocking omission — one your Marketing AI will not make.

We discussed artificial intelligence and the dual meaning of the word *intelligence* in the preface. It means a capacity for thought, but it also means knowledge, a usage you'll recognize from phrases like *military intelligence*. In the SEO arms race, your Marketing AI gives you the intelligence you need to make informed decisions about your SEO, revealing the keywords your competitors rank for, the backlinks they use, and how you can make continual adjustments to improve your ranking. You never own a position in SEO; you only hold it for as long as your pages are the best answer to users' search strings. It's a zero-sum game, and your losses are your competitors' gains. Your Marketing AI helps keep you on top by understanding what your audience truly wants to know and by delivering it to them, effectively shutting the door on the competition.

The specific algorithms that Google, Bing, and Yahoo use to prioritize some sites over others are closely guarded secrets, but for SEO content creators they all boil down to a simple statement: Search engines are built to match as closely as possible with how their users think. These search engines use sophisticated algorithms to think like a user and deliver the closest possible match to a search term. If you're searching for marketing firms in the Pearl River, New York, area, you'd probably type something like "marketing automation Pearl River" into the search bar. By looking at indexed pages that feature incidents of the words *marketing automation* and *Pearl River*, Google delivers relevant results.

How do search engines know to serve you *marketing automation* and *Pearl River* instead of pages that include information about pearls or riverfront property? We'll cover some of the details of source tracking and its importance to your marketing strategy in Chapter 17, but search engines generally use predictive logic and contextual cues on the pages to match what you need as closely as possible. In other words, they use their own form of AI to offer responsive, predictive search results. That's why it's critical to write naturally instead of keyword stuffing or making other attempts to game the system. Using your own AI to understand the ever-changing rules of search engines' AIs is the only way to stay ahead in the eternal arms race.

SEO and SEM

The main focus of this chapter is SEO, which is an integral part of a broader entity: SEM. While SEO is concerned with earning organic traffic, SEM also includes paid search marketing, sponsored links, and advertising. Both organic traffic and paid marketing are vital parts of an overall search engine strategy, and understanding how they differ is essential for creating effective SEO content.

When you look at search results from Baidu, Bing, Google, Yahoo, Yandex, and other search engines, you'll notice a section of sponsored links at the top. Depending on your browser and the search engine you're using, these links may appear in a shaded box, above a line, or with a tag after the name identifying them as paid marketing. Other links related to your search appear on the margin of the page, and these links are sponsored, too, typically at a lower cost than the highly visible links at the top of the results page. SEM includes flat-fee ad links, PPC listings, native advertising content, and the ads served on other pages that relate semantically to a search.

Paid listings are also a valuable research tool for learning about the most effective keywords for SEO. By using paid inclusion and PPC listings, your Marketing AI can refine more precisely your keyword choices and target your audience segments. Because these listings are served according to search terms, you gather essential data about traffic that you can then use to improve your organic search traffic through better, more relevant SEO. Remember, relevance can only happen when you know your audience thoroughly, so your MAI's data discovery, behavioral, and contextual capabilities are critical to guiding your SEO content strategy. Some of the differences between SEO and SEM are illustrated in Table 12.1, and also highlights areas in which they reinforce one another.

SEO as a Moving Target

Users perform more than 100 billion Google searches every month, and that number is constantly growing. The way people use search engines is also evolving; instead of typing in a text string using Boolean logic, users can now say a few words into their smartphones and get results within milliseconds. To understand where SEO is going, it's worth taking a look at where it's been and where Marketing AI is taking it.

In their infancy, Google and other search engines were nowhere near as sophisticated as they are today. They couldn't readily discern keyword stuffing from valuable content and prioritized, high-keyword

SEO	SEM
Brings organic traffic into your website via natural search activity from users	Serves paid listings and advertisements to users
Free to use	Involves an initial investment and/or pay-per-click
Gradually builds traffic over time	Results in immediate traffic
Can be used to build a lasting library that continues to draw visitors	Is useful for rapid keyword analysis to pinpoint areas for future SEO development
Dependent on quality content	Dependent on financial investment and relevant content
User queries are matched to on-site content using keywords and contextual information	User queries are matched to ad copy on click-through destinations
No retargeting strategy	Can use email addresses and tracking pixels to direct retargeting advertisements
Can only use static advertising copy	Can use the retargeting bridge to serve specific ads related to visitors' behavioral, demographic and contextual interests to advance them through their Lead Lifecycle and sales funnel

Table 12.1: SEO/SEM Key Comparisons

counts. This led to a proliferation of sites that relied heavily on keywords and were light on content. For search engine users, these sites devalued the engines that returned such results, so Google and others have spent years refining results with more complex algorithms for determining a site's ranking.

Two of the most important Google changes have been the Panda and Penguin updates. When the first Google Panda update went live in 2011, it altered the face of SEO in ways that are still playing out for content creators and the companies that hire them. Panda targeted low-quality content from mills and sites with high bounce rates, an indication that users weren't finding what they hoped to see on a site. In 2012, Google followed up with the Penguin update, which focused on low-value backlinks and keyword stuffing. These algorithms have gone through major additional updates, but Google and its fellow search engines are constantly adding smaller updates — an estimated 450 to 500 a year. Monitoring these changes and updating pages manually would be a monumental task for a marketing team, but for a Marketing AI, it's a routine process to analyze keyword data and update the marketing team about significant shifts.

Panda, Penguin, and all the hundreds of smaller updates are cumulative; they're permanent gatekeepers to prevent low-value content from swamping the first pages of Google's search results. There's no going back to the days of high keyword density and low-value links. That's great news for businesses that offer high-quality SEO and focus on building authority through good content. You no longer have to compete with low-value content stuffed with high-value keywords to get noticed. But every site owner must pay attention to SEO standards as search engines update them to avoid being caught in a wide net meant to eliminate low-value search results.

AI-governed SEO takes a more holistic, integrated approach than earlier models. It's about monitoring demographic, behavioral, and contextual cues for you and your competition so you can continue to deliver the most relevant — and therefore most highly ranked — information to your prospects. Let's look at some of the ways your site signals that value to search engines and to the people who visit your pages. Your Marketing AI tracks recency, frequency, time-on-page, and other site-quality KPIs to give you a road map to better SEO.

The Building Blocks of SEO

From your information architecture to the tags on your images, everything on your site has the potential to contribute to your SEO strategy. The following seven site elements are some of the most critical areas for optimization.

Tracking Data

Encoded within every site is information that lets site owners learn about visitors. JavaScript codes tell you and your MAI whether a source is organic or from paid search, which search terms the lead used to find you, how frequently a visitor returns, how recently the site was searched, and other key details that create a complete picture of individual leads and the overall performance of your SEO lead-generation strategy.

Title Tags That Work

As its title frequently tells readers what a book is about, a page's title tag indicates to search engines and site visitors what the site contains. Title text automatically displays on search engines, so although it is one of the smallest elements on the page, it may be the single most important line of your text for SEO purposes. Because human readers and search engines alike rely on it to determine a page's relevance, your title text should be optimized for search engines yet clear and compelling to visitors. Titles include all the text that appears between the <title> HTML tags; they should include your company's name and a brief description of what you do.

Meaningful Headers and Subheaders

Organizing content by headers and subheaders helps readers use the site, but search engines also look at these key pieces of information as indicators of the page's purpose. The HTML code on your pages tells search engines which words and phrases are headers, and these headers can be nested to show degrees of importance. Search engines view text between H1 and H2 tags as closely correlated with a site's content. Higher numbers mean smaller subheaders and are considered of lesser relevance. H1 and H2 tags send strong signals to search engines about a site's purpose, so carefully organize your page content.

Valuable Content

Years ago search engines weren't able to rate the quality of content and didn't measure the length of time visitors stayed on a page. They lacked the AI to collect and process the data on these more nuanced signals of site quality and visitor interest. Today, search engine algorithms use a variety of signals to determine a web page's potential value to viewers. Bounce rate — the number of viewers who visit a page and leave immediately — is a strong indicator of quality; a low bounce rate means visitors have found what they wanted, while a high bounce rate is associated with low-value content. A page's "stickiness" — its ability to engage visitors and keep them there — increases its perceived authority in search engine ratings, and sites with higher authority enjoy higher page ranks.

We've stressed the importance of original, well-written content, but we'll say it again: Content your visitors actually want is fundamental to your online marketing success. Creating an original and authoritative library adds to your site's value with every new article or blog post you publish, and great content will lead to greater engagement with your audience with natural backlinks and social media conversations about you.

Your Marketing AI plays a pivotal role in guiding your content strategy, based on behavioral and contextual data from your existing customers, combined with information from site visitors who've reached you via paid or organic searches. A MAS not only collects behavioral data, but also puts it into context to derive meaning from the actions your customers take. Armed with this information, you can know what your audience most wants to see.

Solid Page Performance

Your site can't just look good. It has to perform well, too. Internet connection speeds have become so fast that most users expect the elements on a page to appear instantly. When they encounter a page that takes more than a few seconds to load, they bounce — and as you now know, high bounce rates are not good news for page rankings. Users are also increasingly security aware, and look for sites that treat their data with respect. Poor performance and security concerns will show on your site's traffic metrics within your Marketing AI's analytics dashboard, and sites that perform well often rise to first-page status with search engines.

To gain better page performance (and increase the security of your website), you should take a look at companies like sitelock.com. Sitelock.com reduces the risk of malicious code being injected into your website. In addition, the company maintains a copy of your code, so that in the rare instance a programmer is able to hack into your site, you can quickly restore it to its previous state.

Sitelock.com also offers the advantage of a content distribution network (CDN), a process that significantly improves the user experience with faster load times. A CDN performs this magic by caching the text, graphics, scripts, and media on your website. The costs are reasonable and the impact on your conversion rates can be substantial. Cached graphics and media make the user experience much smoother for returning visitors.

Another important tip that will increase the confidence in your website is to submit your site for rating by Norton (Symantec) Safe Web. By submitting your website, Norton Safe Web validates your website as a safe environment for Internet users by adding a "Norton Secured" checkmark next to your listing in the search engine results page. This seal of approval is an assurance to the prospect that your business has been validated by Norton as a legal business entity and that your website uses Symantec's recommended security practices including best-of-breed SSL Certificates and daily web site malware scanning. For simple, straight forward instructions to get your site validated, point your browser to https://safeweb.norton.com/help/site_owners and follow Norton's directions to have Norton's Secured stamp of approval show up in search results.

Strong Social Media Links

You'll learn more about social media and how to capitalize on its reach in Chapter 13, but here, we focus on the importance of social media for SEO. The rise of social media has revolutionized how search engines assign value to sites. With each wave of updates, search engines give greater weight to value signals from Facebook, Google+, LinkedIn, Twitter, Yelp, and other social networks. Inbound traffic from social media sites suggests that an increasing number of people are seeing the value in your site, and search engines will see it, too. Engaging, shareable content deserves more attention. By taking social media signals of relevance and authority into account, search engines ensure your content gets that bigger audience.

Legitimacy is vital to social media signals in SEO. Real accounts have been around longer and have a higher social reputation than artificial or duplicate accounts. There are no short cuts to having brand advocates. One great way to build your legitimacy and trustworthiness is by being social yourself. Social media is inherently participatory, and reciprocal social links benefit everyone. Forming a link network with your customers, suppliers, colleagues, and industry leaders has more value than simply having a social media presence on a channel without being a part of it.

Make it easy for your visitors to share your latest blog post or feature article via social media to improve your SEO. Even if they love what they've read, hours later your visitors may not remember to share that great piece they read on your blog. Supply them with widgets that let them share instantly on their favorite social media channels. But don't go overboard with choices. Sites that feature two-dozen social media links at the end of every blog post have a lower overall engagement rate than those focusing on the most popular social media platforms. Choose five or six of the most widely used networks, and if you'd like to welcome as much sharing as possible, group the others in a pop-out window.

Domain Age

Established URLs get an authority boost from their longevity. Since Google's early days, millions of websites have gone defunct or have completely changed identities. In such a fluid environment, sites that have stood the test of time typically offer greater value to visitors, and high-value sites rise on search engine results pages. Although your marketing team can't go back a decade to secure and maintain a domain name, it can do the next best thing by remaining steadily active from its inception. Within a few months, a new URL has earned credibility with search engines and can begin to compete on equal footing with older domains.

Understanding Keywords

Keywords, a staple of SEO from the earliest incarnations of user-friendly search engines, are still as important as they ever were, but they're far more complex than simply sprinkling a few related terms into your SEO content. Differentiating between long-tail and short-tail keywords, understanding when and where to use them, comparing your keywords against your competitors', and choosing keywords that match your audience's demographic and contextual data are tasks for a Marketing AI that can crunch the numbers involved.

Changes in the marketplace, your competitors' upgrades, and new search engine algorithms can throw a once-successful keyword engine strategy off balance. A Marketing AI can adjust quickly to advance your position on search engine results pages or maintain your status at the top. In that eternal balancing act, keywords are the single greatest force lifting you up or holding you down, so it's vital to understand how marketing automation and your MAI keep your equilibrium.

Long-Tail versus Short-Tail Keywords

Keyword is a bit of a misnomer because some of the most important keywords aren't single words at all, but phrases. SEO specialists refer to single words and short phrases as short-tail keywords, and the competition for them is white-hot. Unless you're bringing something new to market and have coined an entirely new term for which your audience will likely search, you'll rarely secure high rank for broad, short-tail keywords. These words and short phrases have mass appeal, but the audiences they bring aren't always looking for what you have to offer, leaving you with large traffic volume but less relevance.

Long-tail keywords are detailed, specific phrases that aren't searched as often but are searched by leads that have a good idea of precisely what they want to know. These key phrases are exciting targets for SEO development because they typically correlate closely with knowledgeable prospects that know exactly what they are going to buy.

Since the use of a highly specific keyword phrase is likely to come from serious buyers, long-tail keyword searches are far more likely to convert into a sale. Some may argue that with far fewer searches being made, long-tail keywords do not produce nearly as much traffic, but that disadvantage is compensated for by the benefit of having much less competition, making long-tail keywords far easier to rank for than short-tail phrases.

Here's where a Marketing AI can find that ideal point at which keywords are long enough to be specific yet short enough to be relevant to a larger audience. Again, that point is always changing, particularly in industries that are still in development, such as Marketing AI itself. Let's look at an example of short-tail versus long-tail keywords for SEO Schematics.

The company offers SEO management software for B2B companies, which is fairly specific and that means the AI can discard the broadest short-tail keywords, such as *SEO* and *B2B*. After analyzing past data and looking at source searches, the AI indicates that a few phrases have particularly high involvement: *SEO for B2B* and *B2B SEO software*. People who used these search terms stayed on the site longer and visited more pages, and those behavioral cues suggest high interest. Other long-tail search terms have high-engagement figures, too, but they only get a handful of searches a month. That's not really enough to make these long phrases like *B2B SEO for metal fabrication* a high priority.

The Marketing AI uses all this data to filter search sources and focus on the keywords that hit the sweet spot where search volume and engagement are at their highest — a Goldilocks zone of keywords that are long enough to be relevant but short enough to have broad appeal. With this data in hand, SEO Schematics can focus content on the keywords that have the biggest payoff in terms of interest and volume.

Natural Keywords and Keyword Density

Although keywords aren't the sole determinant of site value that they were in the earliest days of search engine use, they're still essential to any SEO strategy. Whether users type a string of text into a search field or speak a few words into their smartphones, they use keywords without even realizing it. When your site most closely matches those keywords, the search engine returns it as the first result on the page.

Keyword research is its own subspecialty within the SEO industry, and good keyword selection can make or break a site. Including keywords appropriately and naturally reinforces the message of quality and authority all your other SEO signals send. Keywords are powerful, and they require care to use well. Overstuffing content with keywords and raising density beyond about 3 percent can lower a site's credibility with search engines and visitors. Because keyword stuffing is a common tactic for low-value sites that lack the content to build real authority, it can have a serious effect on your page ranking.

A Marketing AI analyzes the keywords you already have on your site, your competitors' keyword use, and visitor source information to build a list of relevant keywords. When your content creation team knows which keywords to target, developing relevant, SEO-friendly content is simplified and produces better-qualified leads. The work your MAI did to create customer profiles also impacts your SEO strategy, allowing you to break out different nurture streams for separate audience segments.

The effectiveness of your keywords in producing qualified leads and conversions is a product of two elements: raw numbers and engagement. Multivariate analysis not only looks at raw traffic data, but also at the degree of engagement each visitor using that keyword has with your site. Some of the engagement signals your AI tracks are time on site, number of pages viewed, and returns to the site. A keyword that has an 80 percent conversion rate seems like an outstanding investment, but if you only get two such keyword searches a month, you probably want to invest modest time and effort there, while focusing on the keyword that delivers a 20 percent conversion rate and receives more than 2,500 hits per month. If even standard SEO practices for lead generation result in a 110 percent ROI, how much more could you do with AI-assisted SEO that maximizes every keyword's effectiveness while minimizing waste?

Keyword-Rich URL Structure

Your site's uniform resource locator (URL) is its virtual address. An address that correlates closely with what your site serves to the public carries more authority with visitors and with search engines. Home page URLs that prominently feature a company's name or the purpose of the page are ideal, but you should use keywords to expand that identity on subordinate pages. With words, names, and hyphens that add detail or clarify a URL, you can come up with something unique and memorable that enhances both your SEO value and your brand identity with the site's visitors. Assign each page its own unique URL instead of developing a site structure that redirects visitors from unrelated pages within the site. Viewers and search engines prefer sites that have a sound logical structure.

When brainstorming your URL text, consider the impact of your naming strategy now and in the future. To create a new page and a unique URL, some companies add the year after the desired text, especially if they're in a hotly competitive industry, but best practices suggest avoiding this method of site building. Adding a date when one isn't needed places an automatic expiration date on the page. Instead, look for ways to incorporate another keyword into your URL. Aim for descriptive text in your URL; like a title, this text string tells viewers what they're going to read on this page, so be as specific as possible.

When creating landing pages and site additions within a marketing automation system, the AI provides automatically generated URLs. These names are usually a good fit, but it's also wise for site developers to double-check the suggested URL to ensure that it makes sense.

Achieving Success with Paid Search

Organic search is essential to increasing site traffic, but it's only one piece of the SEO puzzle. PPC, including native advertising like videos or articles from a paid platform, is both a vital part of SEO and a highly trackable resource for your Marketing AI. PPC is so readily trackable that your AI can act quickly on it to respond by targeting more of your budget to sources that work and limiting resources where the ROI isn't there. The most important tracking parameters to monitor within a destination URL are:

- **Paid search origin:** A visit from a paid search source has a particular code attached: WT.srch=1. Your Marketing AI recognizes searches originating from paid sources by identifying this code

and assigning it to the paid search category. It's the most fundamental piece of information your system collects about a search
source.

- **Program:** Did this search originate from Google AdWords,
Yahoo's Sponsored Search, or another paid search parent
program?

- **Paid keywords:** Which exact terms did you buy, and how has
each term performed? Knowing this data can help you refine
your Marketing AI to connect the prospect with the most relevant content and buying terms that offer the best ROI while
eliminating terms that are a lesser value.

- **Match type:** How closely did the original search term match the
terms you paid for? It's possible to broaden or refine match types
to achieve higher volume or narrow a search to include only the
most highly relevant matches. Possible match types your AI can
monitor include broad matches, exact keyword matches, phrase
matching, content matching, and other advanced options.

- **Source site:** Where did your visitor find the paid search placement? While this is often on a search engine results page itself,
this piece of data can also reveal more about your visitors' sources.

- **Campaign or group ID:** Not all paid searches will include this
data, but if you have set up your Marketing AI to track different
nurture paths, knowing which campaign they belong to is vital.
For example, if SEO Schematics wants to divide inbound search
leads by specific interest, the company can direct its Marketing
AI to tag and route visitors accordingly.

- **Ad copy variations:** For A/B split testing, a topic we'll revisit in
far greater detail within the Analytics section of the book, knowing which ad copy produced the most results is critical.

Just as long-tailed and short-tailed keywords vary in relevance to
different segments of your audience, so can these paid-search factors.
Search origin, search engine, and keywords used are important to all
paid search analytics, but others may not be needed. Group ID, for
example, might be highly relevant to a company with a diverse client
base but unnecessary to one that specializes in serving a specific need for

a single industry. Your AI adjusts to meet your definitions of success, so you and your marketing team can choose which data to include.

Succeeding at SEO: Putting It All Together

Your site must have the total package to reach that first results page and achieve the visibility that brings you new traffic and strengthens your brand identity — something that's easier to achieve with a Marketing AI that gives you a customizable, flexible, and responsive SEO strategy. We've identified these five aspects as the qualities a site must have for successful SEO:

1. **Utility** – Great SEO content means something to your readers and gives them a useful takeaway they can implement for themselves. One of the most important reasons to capture the keyword phrase is to differentiate long tail keywords that are much further along in the buyer's journey. When you connect these prospects to middle- or bottom-of-funnel content, such as white papers, ROI calculators, video testimonials, and pricing, they are far less likely to bounce and more likely to convert into a sale.

   Whether it's a blog post about industry innovations, a press release featuring a new service you offer, or a how-to article on a common problem your customers face, content must contain usable information. Your MAI plays a key role in pinpointing what your audience wants to learn, which in turn drives your SEO content creation to satisfy your viewers. Leave your readers more knowledgeable than they were when they started the article, and you're earning goodwill from search engines as well as from site visitors.

2. **Readability** – Write to your audience to earn more traffic, garner more social media shares and improve your SEO content. Grammar, spelling, and a clean page layout with plenty of white space aren't just frills; they're integral to your SEO efforts. Readability aligns closely with a thorough understanding of your target audience, and your MAI has given you that knowledge. You've built a clear picture of your audience through your

Marketing AI's analytics, and now it's time to serve them the content they deserve.

3. **Authority** – Search engine developers and programmers emphasize the importance of authority when determining how to rank pages. If you're first to market with a major breakthrough in your industry, you have an advantage, but it's challenging to compete with primary sources when you're covering familiar territory. Well-written SEO content helps you establish your own territory on which you're an authority. Remember, SEO is a zero sum game. You need to know the lay of the land your competition currently holds. This is something you gain from your MAI's keyword data on your competitor's rankings. By using that knowledge to your advantage and creating authoritative content with optimal keyword choices, you position yourself as the best source of information for a knowledge-hungry public. Authority leads to visibility, and visibility leads to more traffic.

4. **Specificity** – Building in localization and specialization is an excellent way to own your share of a market. Your site almost certainly faces stiff competition on a national level, but as the only local provider of a key product or service, your organization can more easily move into the preferred position regionally by addressing your local customers' needs.

5. **Relevance** – Search engines and readers alike look for keywords and backlinks that make sense. Relevant links, meaningful keywords, and interdependent pages ensure high relevance to visitors whether they've arrived there via organic or paid search. Synonyms send strong signals to search engines about your site's purpose and how it should be categorized, enhancing its overall relevance. Your Marketing AI's search source data is incredibly valuable for pinpointing and promoting relevant keywords. As we noted earlier, you can't be relevant to your audience until you know who they are, so this aspect of your SEO relates back to your discovery process.

SEO isn't all that mysterious. Once you put the pieces together, it's a very logical process. It's all about great content, sound site architecture, and matching the right keyword to the right prospect at the right time. Your Marketing AI can make search engines acknowledge and promote your site by supplying what their users want most. Social media can also have a dramatic impact on your SEO. In Chapter 13, you'll learn how to optimize its use and create a conversation with your prospects and customers.

Takeaways:

1. Words are the key to SEO, so be selective and carefully chose each one.
2. Content, page structure, and linking fuel effective SEO.
3. Use SEM to pave the way for your SEO strategy.

CHAPTER 13

SOCIAL MEDIA

We're a social species, and the networks that let us broadcast our opinions, ideas, and reviews instantaneously also let us indulge the urge to share. Social media is about more than sharing personal anecdotes and photos; it's a powerful, motivating force for driving traffic toward companies that use it effectively and for nurturing brand advocates. On average, over 80 percent of your customers regularly use some form of social media. It's imperative to tap into that market and speak to your customers where they're listening. A Marketing AI is able to take that uniquely human habit of sharing thoughts and use it to inform marketing decisions, picking up on and amplifying social signals to help you remain relevant to your audience.

Many marketers stumble over social media when directly trying to monetize it. Unlike other marketing channels, such as PPC and banners, social media isn't solely for ads. Through it, your prospects can enter your sales funnel in new ways and bring more knowledge with them when they come to you. Knowing what social media can and can't do for your AI-enhanced marketing strategy will let you make the most of this powerful tool.

The challenge for social media marketing has been locating your audience in the huge volume of people who use social channels. With billions of users, how do you find your target audience in the crowd? Using real-time personalization and retargeting via your Marketing AI, what initially looks like a problem becomes the solution. A Marketing AI can identify the people on social networks who have already interacted with you among those undifferentiated billions, letting you concentrate your ad spending on engaged qualified leads.

The Social Sales Funnel

The traditional concept of the sales funnel is still useful in marketing, but social media has changed it dramatically. Leads come into the funnel far more educated, and social media provides one of the avenues through which they educate themselves. Whether they participate in a conversation about you on Facebook or LinkedIn or read a glowing review on Yelp, they're leveraging other customers' experiences to make their own buying decisions. Traditionally, the top of the funnel consisted of leads that were still learning about you and were still undifferentiated. Your team would then perform a needs assessment on this large group of prospects to locate the smaller group of leads within that large mass, and then focus marketing efforts on a select pool of marketing accepted leads.

In that traditional model, increasing the flow at the base of the funnel typically meant broadening it at its top, looking farther afield for new markets. With the rise of email marketing, search engines, crowd-sourced reviews, and social media governed by a Marketing AI that coordinates omni-channel marketing to an unprecedented degree, that simplified model is obsolete. Prospects enter your sales funnel already fairly educated about your company and what it offers. The modern sales funnel is porous, admitting entry throughout its length and not just from its top.

Here's why this matters for social media: Social channels operate at every level of the Lead Lifecycle, but it's impossible to coordinate marketing at every level of the sales funnel without a Marketing AI to manage it. Sending AI-assisted marketing messages across all social media channels encourages your prospects to explore more on their own, bringing themselves further into your sales funnel and engaging on a deeper level. Meanwhile, your MAI collects essential data about your leads from every social media channel, turning every conversation into knowledge you can convert directly into revenue. One of the greatest challenges of social media — quantifying its contribution to revenue — is solved with Marketing AI.

You learned earlier about the importance of tracking prospects while they're still anonymous and then later tying that anonymous data to known leads. In a social media context that ability presents an even greater opportunity for discovery. Anonymous prospects whose trajectories you trace with a tracking pixel can be retargeted on their social networks, giving them offers of gated content that encourage them to reveal their information and turn them into known leads.

For known leads that have already shared their information with you, tracking and retargeting on social media (in addition to other marketing channels) lets you serve even more finely calibrated and closely targeted content to guide their progress along the Lead Lifecycle. By reaching these leads in a social media environment, you make it effortless to share their knowledge of your brand. Email contact can encourage them to forward to a friend, but social media contact allows them to immediately reach all their friends with a single retweet or Facebook post.

AI-Assisted B2B Marketing in Social Media

Some B2B marketers mistakenly assume social media is largely for B2C sales, but while conversations about the latest consumer electronics or fashion trend can certainly drive interest on social media, those discussions are only a fraction of the conversation going on. Customer bases in B2B sales are smaller but deeper; your clients know more about their industry, make bigger buys, and influence purchases from other departments within their organization. Approval for purchases is multilayered, and people communicate with one another at each buying-authority tier, often in the relatively public forum of social media.

A good portion of B2B sales comes from your customers' perceptions of your trustworthiness, and social media is an excellent way to foster that trust. Through Facebook, Google +, and Twitter, you can answer their questions directly. LinkedIn lets you create a profile to showcase your bona fides in the business realm. YouTube and Vimeo provide a platform for how-to videos and demonstrations of your product. All these points of connection with your prospects build your industry authority and demonstrate your willingness to be there for your customers.

The ability to track leads both anonymously and after learning more information about them is critical to B2B marketing, much of which is heavily dependent on finding a tightly focused market among a large volume of messages. B2B audiences tend to be narrow but deep; once you tap into them they lead to more high-value prospects through referrals and shared information. That makes social media retargeting a perfect fit, because reaching one lead with relevant information so often leads directly to finding other prospects with it, too.

Quantifying Social Signals

The importance of social media in marketing is obvious, but unless you have the right tools, measuring its impact and relating it to revenue is not. With a Marketing AI to measure engagement, monitor social-media lead sources, track anonymous and known prospects as they share knowledge about you, qualify leads, and place them on the appropriate nurture track, you turn the strength of social signals into real revenue. Social media contacts and retargeting help speed leads' transition from phase to phase within the Lead Lifecycle while feeding your Marketing AI data about new prospects to contact via social sharing.

A Marketing AI also assigns specific values to the leads you gain through social media, showing your marketing team where to focus its efforts and where it can pare unnecessary costs. You might get huge volumes of traffic from Facebook and relatively few from LinkedIn, for example, but if those LinkedIn visitors have higher engagement metrics, your Marketing AI prioritizes them as they offer a better ROI than the larger audience.

But this doesn't mean that your large Facebook audience is lost. Because Marketing AI technology excels at determining leads' interests and allocating resources, you're able to gain real value from these leads over time. By assigning social engagement data to specific leads' records, you have detailed information about the lead's source, keywords or hashtags that initiated activity, and how often the lead engages with you. Once your Marketing AI gathers and compiles this information, it's able to start that prospect on the appropriate nurture track. These activity logs stay with a customer's records, too, so these social media cues stay relevant throughout the lifetime of your customer relationships as they evolve from anonymous prospects to known leads.

Following are just some of the questions your Marketing AI answers for you — and the answers convert directly into revenue:

- Which social media messages get shared, pinned, or retweeted?
- What's your largest source of social media leads, and is it the same channel that provides the leads with the highest level of engagement?
- Which social media channels contribute additional leads through social sharing?
- Which posts and tweets get the most positive attention?
- How does your social media strategy intersect with your email marketing, SEO, and content marketing?
- Which hashtags get you the most attention?
- How familiar is your social media audience with you, and what can you do to increase that familiarity?

Matching Your Message to Your Media

The discoveries your AI makes about your leads through anonymous browser cookies and exploration of social media links also serve you well in this phase of the marketing cycle. Knowing where to send a message is as important as the message itself. Your MAI's discovery process tells you where to focus your efforts even before you create your company profile on a social media channel. Social media is free, but advertising on it is not, so it's imperative to understand where and how you should spend your time on each of the major social media channels. Remember, you aren't trying to reach all the people all the time — you want to reach the right people at the right time. In a sea of billions of users, your MAI pinpoints your audience and serves it directly with the content it finds most relevant through real-time personalization, so you deliver uniquely relevant messages at the right point of the Lead Lifecycle to guide your future customers along their buyers' journeys.

Your Marketing AI also tracks the rise and fall of engagement on social media platforms over time, revealing potential new markets and areas for growth within existing audience segments. Small fluctuations tell you about the relative popularity of individual campaigns, but long-term changes give you critical information about the overall strength of your social signal. The ability to speak to people who have already engaged with your brand on a platform where you know they're listening is an invaluable retargeting tool.

The social media networks list below is necessarily incomplete. New social networks are founded every day, and no one can predict which ones will be big hits. Former giants like Friendster and MySpace are either defunct or serve niche markets now, and although the major players are unlikely to fade from the scene completely, they also change over time. Instead, this overview provides insight into the best fit for types of social media channels. Here, too, your Marketing AI is invaluable, giving you data that reveals which social media channels are highly correlated with your audience, which are robust, and which are on the wane in your industry. Marketing automation systems can track lead data across multiple social media platforms at once, and allow your MAI team to add new ones as needed.

Facebook

Social media giant Facebook has more than 1.3 billion users worldwide, more than 750 million of whom are daily users. That's a potentially vast market for any company; for B2B industries that traditionally have smaller customer bases, it's vital to find your audience in the crowd. Because Facebook allows rapid, concise communication between customers and businesses, it's a good way to answer customer questions, especially if you feel others might have similar questions.

For companies that want to establish their brand and create a stronger identity, Facebook is a cornerstone of brand building. The Facebook Timeline feature lets visitors look deeper into where a company has been as well as where it's headed, adding value to past marketing campaigns as they continue to contribute to current perceptions. Having a sense of who you are over time also makes customers more willing to place their trust in you in the future, so establishing your Facebook presence early and maintaining it over time pays indirect dividends, as well. Good uses for Facebook include:

- Fostering name recognition
- Establishing brand identity
- Giving your MAI deeper insight into leads' interests
- Communicating with customers and prospects
- Reaching your target audience within a vast sea of names
- Gathering behavioral and contextual data
- Being available where most customers can easily find you

Twitter

Of companies using social media, 85 percent are on Twitter. But not all Twitter use is equal and having a presence on a social media channel is not the same as maximizing its value. Your Marketing AI gives you a way to turn retweeting into pathways to new leads, maximizing the impact of every tweet you make. Twitter's distinguishing characteristic is its speed.

The rapidly growing social network also makes it easy to share and organize content via hashtags, those one-line identifiers preceded by a # sign. When visitors want information about a given topic, they search using hashtags as keywords, giving companies that use the same hashtag easy entry into the conversation. That makes good hashtag use a tremendously effective technique for building brand awareness, but it also leads to links that aren't always intuitive, which potentially opens your audience to a wider range of prospects. Hashtags are an outstanding way to gain entry into conversations that have particular relevance for your audience and give you ready access to new leads as your current leads share and tag your content.

Because Twitter is highly interactive, it lets you communicate with followers in real-time. Visitors who have questions can get answers right away, which in turn demonstrates your commitment to customer service — a key aspect of success. Retweeting lets customers carry useful information farther with no increased investment on your part. Twitter also serves well as a form of headline news for other media you publish. By tweeting a link to your latest blog post or Facebook update, you encourage Twitter followers to drill deeper into your site or establish contact with you via other means. Ways to make the most of your Twitter account include:

- Increasing name recognition
- Reaching new prospects via hashtags
- Updating visitors conveniently and concisely about your latest news
- Responding to queries on the fly
- Giving leads insider knowledge with content that moves them along the Lead Lifecycle
- Building rapport with customers and prospects

Google+

Google is a titan among search engines, but its social media channel, Google+, is still in its youth. It's growing quickly and opens avenues to highly engaged audiences for companies that invest time in it. Establishing a presence on multiple social networks is a sound strategy, and Google+ should be at the top of any B2B company's list because of its business-friendly design. The Google+ Communities feature lets companies register and operate as brands; some older social media channels have had to adapt to business and corporate uses. High-value leads self-select to join communities that speak to their interests and by joining those communities as a provider, you become uniquely accessible to them and can use your MAI's tracking capabilities to find more like them.

Circles, the way Google+ organizes how its users connect with one another, easily map to your MAI's market segmentation. By placing visitors in different circles, you can communicate with each segment individually or speak to everyone at once, then reinforce these selective messages with real-time personalization. That increased flexibility can also enhance split-variable testing programs, making your future marketing campaigns more effective.

Primary uses for Google+ include:

- Connecting with a self-selected audience of interested prospects
- Delivering highly specific retargeting messages
- Communicating in-depth with customers and leads
- Using your MAI's analytics to understand your audience
- Defining new audience segments
- Refining your marketing efforts through testing

LinkedIn

The premier social media platform for business and corporate interests is a natural home for B2B social media marketing. While the network is smaller than its higher-profile counterparts, LinkedIn users are almost exclusively business-oriented, making it a valuable platform for your MAI's retargeting and RTP programs. More than half the people in the LinkedIn system have decision-making capability, so connecting with them means connecting with your potential buyers.

LinkedIn gives you powerful profile tools, allowing you to post video, images, and text that tell visitors far more about your company than a simple form could. An extensive and customizable profile option helps you create, maintain, and control your reputation within the network. The links your vendors, customers, and prospects supply connect with your profile page to give new leads the best possible look at your company. Tools unique to LinkedIn, particularly SlideShare, let you repurpose informational content from other marketing venues for LinkedIn. As an idea exchange, SlideShare is especially exciting, allowing you to communicate a great deal of information in a small space. When creating your LinkedIn profile, use the platform primarily for:

- Defining your brand for B2B and corporate clients
- Participating in relevant interest groups to establish authority

- Giving back publicly to a community by answering questions
- Generating high-quality leads
- Displaying recommendations from other users as social proof

YouTube

YouTube users view billions of videos a day, and they aren't all cat videos or movie trailers. Businesses use YouTube as a means to connect with their audience, show a behind-the-scenes glimpse of how the company operates, offer product demonstrations, or bring multimedia conferences to a wider audience. Video content is instantly engaging to viewers, and YouTube makes it easy to distribute that content. Data gleaned from YouTube is especially valuable to your Marketing AI because it functions both as a social media channel and as a search engine. Through analysis of YouTube data, an MAI is able to place leads precisely within the Lead Lifecycle and deliver highly relevant RTP content by retargeting ads served to these viewers when they visit other sites or channels on the Google Display Network.

The ability to search YouTube is another reason to invest in it. Using titles, descriptions, and on-page content with your videos is a key component of your SEO strategy. Popularity ratings can also propel your videos to higher rankings on search engine–results pages. Inbound links, including links from sites that embed your video, increase search engine standings, as well. Adding outbound links to video descriptions or with in-picture linking can in turn lift the target pages to higher prominence. Some key ways to use YouTube include:

- Showing viewers valuable information instead of telling them
- Demonstrating products, processes, and services
- Letting prospects learn more about your company and its personnel
- Enhancing SEO
- Establishing a clearer brand identity
- Generating organic publicity about your organization
- Retargeting viewers visiting other sites or channels on the Google Display Network

Developing Your Social Media Presence

Social media channels serve a number of business purposes, including direct communication with your audience, lead generation, and data collection. No matter how you use it, your social media presence needs branding as surely as your website, blog, and landing pages do. Standing out is pivotal to using social media well, but social media shouldn't become an echo chamber in which everyone sees one innovator's success and tries to borrow its cachet. Your Marketing AI's analytics help you stay ahead of your competitors here.

Entertainment should be one goal of your social media interactions, but it's only part of the picture. You also want to educate, inform, share observations, and listen to your customers based on their stage in the Lead Lifecycle. Not every brand has to use the same marketing voice, and not every company should define itself against its biggest competitors. It's always better to know who your customers are and speak in the voice that's natural to your organization. Finding that voice often involves some deliberation and discovery. Is your brand altruistic? Green? Service-oriented? Innovative? Localized? Custom-crafted? Whatever defines you should also inform your social media presence.

Tips for Using AI-Assisted Social Media

Social media channels are not free advertising space; they're opportunities for conversations. If you're delivering an ad-heavy monologue that focuses solely on your company, you can't attract the followers and fans necessary to make your social media strategy a success. Instead, offer insights, solutions, actionable information, anecdotes, and questions that attract visitors whom you know have an interest in what you're saying. Your MAI can then track these visitors as they interact on social media channels and lead you to more potential leads.

Engagement is key, but a steady stream of ads doesn't engage your prospects. Your AI measures engagement by tracking where leads come from, how long they spend on site, how many pages they view, and other behavioral details that it then places in context. With that knowledge, your MAI is able to deliver RTP content that guides leads farther along the sales pipeline.

✓ **Be everywhere**. Social media channels are meant to intercon-
nect, not act in isolation. Your Facebook page, Google+ groups,
LinkedIn profile, SlideShare portfolio, Twitter feed, and
YouTube library can all cross-reference one another to build a
self-referring web that ensures your prospects find what they want
to know no matter where they encounter you. Your AI then monitors their movements across channels, building a clearer picture
of where your words have the most resonance. Keeping all these
channels up to date and coordinated with the rest of your omni-
channel marketing strategy by hand would be an exhausting task
for a human marketer, but an AI effortlessly orchestrates your
social media marketing.

✓ **Make yourself useful**. Message boards and forums give you the
chance to help, and the visitor you help today could be tomorrow's customer. Others can also see you participating in the community, becoming more familiar with your brand and associating
your company with subject knowledge and active involvement.
Social media channels that let you interact with your leads and
customers are valuable media streams; make the most of them.
Set alerts within your MAI, and your marketing or sales team
can get instantaneous updates whenever someone comments,
forwards a link, or asks a question.

✓ **Use collected data wisely**. Social media is an excellent way for
learning more information about your visitors both through site
analytics and through response pages or surveys. With it, you're
able to find additional leads while you get a clearer idea of what
your known leads need to progress through the Lead Lifecycle.
The data you amass can be tremendously valuable to your marketing team's analysts and help your Marketing AI steer future
marketing campaigns too.

✓ **Include content marketing in your social media strategy**. Without
content, you have little to say on your social media channels, but
by regularly updating your blog, releasing informative feature
articles, and posting new content to other social media streams,
you have a wealth of reasons to tweet.

Once you've built your social media strategy to reinforce your brand identity and connect with customers, it's time for those conversations to lead your prospects where you want them to go. In Chapter 14 you'll learn how to bring social engagement online into offline venues as you guide leads farther along your sales pipeline with trade shows and webinars.

Takeaways:

1. Social media is more than sharing photos — it drives traffic to your site and builds your brand.
2. Proper analytics are required to determine the true value of social media to your bottom line.
3. Your social strategy should not be focused on a particular outlet, but on a consistent voice that transcends each of them.

CHAPTER 14

Tradeshows and Webinars

Tradeshows have been a marketing staple for about as long as marketing has existed. The idea of gathering with other merchants to display your wares is a venerable one, but the modern tradeshow no longer has to take place in person, nor does it have to involve a physical commodity. Webinars let you demonstrate your product line, showcase your services, and educate your audience remotely. Even better, when you offer webinars for download they let you do these things before a new audience each time. In this chapter, you'll learn how to turn tradeshows and webinars from costly propositions into lead generators and revenue builders.

Why Tradeshows Still Matter

When Internet marketing first took off, some marketers predicted that it would spell the death of the tradeshow. In fact, research suggests the opposite: the Bureau of Labor Statistics estimates an annual growth of 4.8 percent in exhibition-industry revenue. Tradeshows have plenty of attendees: An estimated 200 million people attend tradeshows annually. For B2B industries, these exhibitions are even more important because the buying cycle is so much longer and more involved. Attendees on average spend more than nine hours at an exhibition, which gives you plenty of time to make an impact on people while they're engaged with you. The people at a tradeshow are there because they already have a baseline interest in what you have to say, making them exceptional leads to nurture. When you could spend months on closing a single sale, it makes sense to invest time and money into these leads.

Like direct mail, tradeshows are an arena in which you can stake out your own territory without as much competition. Setting up for a tradeshow or conference takes an investment that many companies aren't willing to make, despite tradeshows' proven track record of delivering a high ROI on every lead. That reluctance works to your advantage, especially when you have a Marketing AI that will make the most of every lead, routing the lead to the appropriate nurture track and delivering the right content at the right time throughout the Lead Lifecycle.

Tradeshows also give you and your Marketing AI unrivaled access to your prospects' information, and you get it straight from the source. Most tradeshows allow you to scan an attendee's badge to gain access to the individual's contact information and corporate profile. Tradeshows and webinars are ideal places to seek contact information for all forms of communication, and it's as simple as asking, "May we scan your badge so we can send you more information?" Considering that 80 percent of tradeshow attendees have buying authority, that's information you and your Marketing AI need to know.

Tradeshows provide the best possible opportunity to capture your leads' data to put all this information into a larger contextual framework. In many cases, your lead nurturing begins with the preshow list that features attendees' names, email addresses, and other demographic and firmographic data. During the show, you also get additional information from leads who stop by your booth and interact with you, letting you fill customer profiles with more detailed data that then becomes part of your Marketing AI's knowledge base.

This matters because it's that bigger picture that shows you where these leads are along their buying journey and where your AI places them along the appropriate nurture track. Because they've already ventured out to a tradeshow, they're interested in something at that exposition; your MAI's nurture track is able to treat them as individuals, giving them what they need to know to buy from you.

Because you can build brand awareness, generate highly qualified and motivated leads, and build better relationships with your potential customers, it's easy to see why tradeshows are still great investments. The power of Marketing AI drives your tradeshow ROI higher, provides each lead what it needs to reach the end of the buyer's journey, makes an already valuable event essential to your revenue-marketing strategy, and delivers a nurtured, ready-to-buy prospect to your sales team's door.

Tradeshows and the Lead Lifecycle

Like any element of your marketing strategy, tradeshows lend themselves well to audience segmentation by demographic, firmographic, behavioral, and contextual data. You already have some information about leads at a tradeshow from the fact that they're there at all (a strong behavioral signal of interest), and from their attendance. Let's take a look, then, at how your Marketing AI ranks leads generated from tradeshows and puts those rankings in the context of the Lead Lifecycle.

Your Marketing AI sets up three possible progressions (levels of engagement), each of which has its own nurture track:

1. **Attendees** – Just by having attended a tradeshow, prospects have an ideal customer profile and are promising recipients of your marketing content. This group includes everyone who signed up for the tradeshow, and these leads count as marketing-accepted leads. They're in the general neighborhood of your target audience, but they need some screening and nurturing before they're ready for more in-depth information. Your Marketing AI uses this information to send engaging email invitations to enter a drawing to win a free prize, receive a free consultation, or see a demonstration of your product.

2. **Booth Visitors** – These leads not only attended the exposition but also stopped by your booth to pick up literature, scan their ID card, or drop a business card in a prize jar. Because you know they stopped at your booth, you and your Marketing AI can assume they know your brand and something about you. At this point, these leads roughly parallel the MQL stage of the Lead Lifecycle. By using this information, it continues the nurture process by sending a follow-up email thanking them for their

interest and entering them into the weekly MQL-email nurture stream.

3. **Engaged Leads** – People who take the time to talk to your representative at the tradeshow know enough about you to actively seek out more information. They're highly engaged with your brand, and depending on the conversation you have with them, they may be sales-accepted or sales-qualified leads (SAL and SQL on the Lead Lifecycle chart in Chapter 5). These are more than prospects, they're opportunities. Your AI assists by *immediately* sending an email, thanking them for their time and scheduling a follow up call to close the sale.

It's this third level of engagement that counts as a success to your MAI. Until leads reach that point, they're placed in the appropriate nurture track designed to supply them with the content they need to get there. By the time your representative speaks with a lead at a tradeshow, your MAI has already amassed a great deal of information about that person so you can give relevant answers and guide the conversation.

You can have meaningful conversations with prospects, even if you haven't met them face to face, by using webinars, which generate between 20 and 40 percent of B2B companies' leads — it's critical to handle them well. From preregistration to sign-ups to the event itself to future downloads from new leads, a Marketing AI turns an already vital aspect of your revenue marketing strategy into a lead-generation machine.

MAI-Assisted Webinars

In a sense, webinars are like online tradeshows without any other vendors. You know attendees already have significant interest in what you're offering. With this channel you get in-depth data on leads and have a chance to speak directly to your audience. As with tradeshows, you guide the conversation, but in this case you do it remotely. Moreover, you get to do it repeatedly because webinars last for as long as you have them recorded and available on your website. You're only able to attend a tradeshow once, but a webinar can funnel well-prepared, highly qualified leads to your sales team time after time.

Your Marketing AI not only collects data on webinar sign-ups and attendees, it also administers every step of the information flow before, during, and after the webinar (and delivers new attendees who sign up for the webinar to the appropriate point of the marketing pipeline). In Chapter 5 we discussed the importance of behavioral and contextual data when scoring leads in other channels, and that data is just as vital regarding webinars. The difference is, a lot of that data flows into the system in real-time, and only a Marketing AI can keep pace. To get an idea of how a Marketing AI manages a webinar, let's go through the steps of creating, promoting, delivering, and following up on one.

Choosing a Webinar Topic

Too many companies spend their time and money creating webinars that focus on what they want to say, rather than on what their audience wants to hear, and then wonder why they have such small audiences. A Marketing AI that has carefully tracked demographic, firmographic, behavioral, and contextual data over time will show you where your audience's interests lie. The keyword analysis you do for your SEO also applies here, steering you to the topics your visitors search most frequently. Demographic and firmographic information tells you who your potential webinar audience is so you can directly address their needs. When brainstorming webinar subjects, looking at the data your MAI has already amassed will dramatically streamline the process.

Webinar Promotion

If your audience doesn't know about your webinar it can't sign up for it. Blog posts and guest posts, newsletters, tradeshows, Facebook events, LinkedIn groups, front page banners, email invitations — all of these are prime opportunities to let people know what they'll be getting.

Your AI knows which audience segments each of your marketing channels reaches and will guide your promotion strategy. For example, website visitors who find you via an organic search might respond best to a home page banner that features a mention of the keywords they used to find you — and yes, you can customize home pages within your marketing automation system, a process we'll describe in Chapter 15. Your newsletter recipients may respond better to an in-depth article that feeds their desire for more knowledge about the subject of your webinar.

The Marketing AI also simplifies forms setups. Make it easy for attendees to participate by letting them sign up via Facebook, Twitter, an on-site form, or a custom landing page reached through a link in email. These forms serve a dual purpose: They reserve space for attendees, of course, but they also give your MAI a wealth of new data on leads. As people fill in the blanks, your marketing automation system cross-references and stores the information within each lead's profile. You're also able to filter responses; by requiring a business email address for sign-ups, for example, you remove people who are unlikely to become customers from your attendance list.

After prospects fill out the necessary reservation forms, your MAI also initiates an email sequence that starts with an autoresponder thank-you message. This note is a small but critical step because it verifies your lead's information and serves as a reminder to attend — and you do want attendance, not just sign-ups. Your MAI knows who has signed up and knows who hasn't. Therefore, it will continue to communicate reasons to register to your non-respondent audience and send a reminder to attend to current registrants. As the optimal numbers of emails are delivered, the AI will manage each email deployment. The importance of registering and then attending is extremely high. We find that when a registrant attends one of our webinars she is about 60 percent more likely to become a customer than a registrant that didn't attend, so you don't want them to miss out on the presentation.

Should a lead register for a webinar and not attend, you still have a chance to make an impact on that lead. Allowing registrants who miss the webinar to download a recording of the event from a third-party source affords you an excellent opportunity to ask for more information and to refine that lead's qualification status.

Execution

Even with a thank-you for signing up, attendees sometimes forget about a scheduled webinar without the occasional reminder. Depending on how far out the event is, your AI schedules an email reminder a week in advance and another the day of the webinar. Timing of reminders varies from industry to industry and person to person. As with every aspect of your marketing strategy, your MAI can track historical data and reveal what the most effective reminder schedule is for your audience.

From your Marketing AI's standpoint, the webinar itself is the easy part. It records attendance, tracks whether people stay for the entire presentation, and prepares an autoresponder thank-you message for attendees. A marketing automation system also integrates with popular webinar software to create and organize slides for a sleek, compelling presentation. If your webinar's presented live, allot enough time for audience questions; if it's recorded, consider implementing a chat messaging service that lets new attendees communicate directly with your representatives.

Webinar Follow-Up

A timely, organized follow-up after your webinar delivers higher conversion rates, and an MAI excels at coordinating follow-ups and reminders. Your first step is one you've already read — sending a thank-you via autoresponder. You and your marketing team can choose to send out a general thank you to all attendees, but you can also fine-tune the responses to send different messages to leads depending on what questions they asked in the Q&A or how long they stayed with the webinar. Historically, attendees who stay for the entire event have far greater conversion rates than those who leave early, so your AI sends a direct mail offer and arranges a telemarketing call as part of the follow-up process on these highly qualified leads.

Having tracked the behavioral and contextual cues from attendees during every step of the process, your MAI has also been scoring these leads so it can channel them toward the correct nurture flow. Some leads may have reached the SAL or even SQL stages by the end of the webinar, while others need additional input to arrive at that point. Either way, your marketing automation system can schedule emails and phone calls to maximize the ROI on every webinar lead.

Sorting and Scoring

Some of your most valuable leads come from tradeshows and webinars, yet the cost of procuring and nurturing these leads is higher than it is for many other marketing channels. To keep the return on your investment of time and money as high as possible, it's imperative to put verified, qualified leads on the appropriate nurture track, while weeding out false signals of interest. It would be impossible for a human on your marketing team to go through all your records, cross-reference them with attendee records, eliminate dead ends, and put valid leads on the right nurture program. For your Marketing AI, it's a routine task.

A certain number false signals appear in tradeshow and webinar attendee lists as students and members of the press. Although they're there to learn about you, that knowledge rarely translates into sales. Often, would-be leads are competitors who want to see what they're up against or learn a few new ideas. Even the friendliest competition will never buy from you, and your marketing automation system knows that. It's able to spot these false signals and filter these results out of the nurture process so you aren't handing your competition tools they could use to leverage their own success.

When people sign up for a webinar or tradeshow, they're already sending a strong signal of interest, but sometimes it's a challenge to see just where that interest lies. Let's take a look at SEO Schematics for a quick example. The company has landed a booth at FOLIO, an annual publishers convention. The tradeshow draws tens of thousands of attendees ranging from content marketers to website developers, but only some of them will be specifically interested in the SEO software solutions the company provides. SEO Schematics' Marketing AI can filter attendees by interest, demographic data, and firmographic information. By filtering leads by score and sorting the most promising prospects into differentiated nurture streams, the company is able to turn every possible lead into a sale and maximize every dollar it spent on attending the tradeshow.

In this chapter we discussed customized home pages, and in Chapter 8 you learned about personalization. Next, in Chapter 15, you'll see how we put these elements together for a wholly customized experience. With

MAI, you're able to deliver personalized landing pages, white papers, and other content at every step of the Lead Lifecycle.

Takeaways:

1. Trade show attendees are typically in the later stages of the buyer's journey.
2. Exhibiting at trade shows offer a unique opportunity to present a more in-depth value proposition to multiple prospects.
3. If your webinar content speaks to your audience's interests, the value to your brand will be undeniable.

CHAPTER 15

WEBSITES AND LANDING PAGES

From your email marketing and creative to your social media presence, many of your MAI's communications have an underlying goal: to move prospects farther down the marketing funnel and closer to a sale. To achieve that goal, your email blasts, blog posts, and tweets have links that lead to landing pages or to relevant pages on your corporate website. When they arrive, prospects need to experience a page that fits with and furthers your brand identity. The page must also be functional, relevant, targeted, and concise. That's a tall order for a single page, but in this chapter you'll read how to develop website content and landing pages that fill these needs and more.

What a Landing Page Is

To those who aren't familiar with online marketing, any page could be called a landing page, but to marketers, it's a far more specific entity. Your landing page is where visitors wind up after clicking a link or typing in a URL from any of your other marketing channels, and you aren't limited to one. In fact, savvy marketers frequently use numerous landing-page designs to test campaigns' effectiveness or monitor their reach. The print-magazine reader who sees your offer in an ad, the newsletter subscriber who wants to learn more about your latest product line, and the blog visitor who found your page through Google should be directed to subtly different landing pages personalized to their target audience.

With marketing automation, you're able to deliver fully customized landing pages to each visitor based on information you've already learned about that visitor — even if you don't yet know your prospect's name. In Chapter 3 we discussed how anonymous browser cookies let your Marketing AI link data attached to a particular IP address, and nowhere is that knowledge more directly useful than when delivering customized landing-page content. Using behavioral and contextual data, your AI already has an idea of what that prospect wants to see and serves website content and landing pages that relate to previous behavior.

Your site's visitors may browse any page on your website, but the landing page is that first point of contact with the business end of your site. Prospects who are engaged enough to click through an email call to action or a link in your blog post have already signaled that they want to see more; your landing page is designed to convince them to take the next step. After putting in all the work to gather information, develop brilliant creative, build a better blog, and implement solid SEO strategies to help new prospects find you, your landing page translates that interest into action.

Your landing pages are designed with action in mind. As a result, they include a form on which visitors can take that action. It may be an order form for a sample or new product, a subscription form, a request for quotes, or a data form for a free download. Throughout *Marketing AI: From Automation to Revenue Performance Marketing*, we've stressed how important your prospects' data is, and the forms on your landing pages are excellent ways to collect that information. Your MAI links that data with the information already collected, including behavioral and contextual data from your lead's earliest anonymous visits, to create a complete image of each lead. From there, the AI is able to route leads to the proper place along the sales pipeline and start delivering the right content to them.

A good landing page is more than just a form, though. It gives you one more chance to tell visitors why they should take that next step with you. A bullet-point summary of what they'll receive for subscribing or why they should take advantage of the offer that convinced them to click through serves as a powerful reinforcement of your message. It's also another key area for branding, so keep your look and message consistent on landing pages; the landing page is close to the finish line, but a campaign can still falter if its message or design is off-brand. Pages designed within your marketing automation system can be thematically linked with ease, keeping your site on-brand.

What a Landing Page Isn't

- **Generic**. A landing page is highly specific and designed for a particular course of action, so unless you're using marketing automation to deliver customized web pages, you aren't achieving the specificity and actionability of a landing page. Visitors may "land" on your home page, especially if they find you via search engines thanks to your strong SEO strategy, but that doesn't make it a landing page.
- **Overcrowded**. A landing page serves a single, well-defined purpose. Instead of broadening an individual page's scope (making it too general), a better solution is to add a new landing page for a different purpose. For example, if you're looking for newsletter subscribers and link a landing page from your blog, you want to create a separate landing page for blog readers who want to request your latest white paper. Creating separate landing pages also gives you far more fine-grained behavioral and contextual data that your Marketing AI can then use to score and guide leads.
- **Plain**. A landing page generally contains a form, but it should be more than just a few lines where visitors can place their order. Every step you ask your prospects and customers to take is another step at which they can opt out of the process, so add some content to remind them why they should stay the course.
- **Disorganized**. You've led your visitors to the landing page, but they must be able to find the information they want at a glance. Above-the-fold content, clear headlines, itemized lists, and easy-to-use forms are imperative. Leave plenty of white space on the page to ensure that everything you write has maximum impact. Remember, visitors have already done a fair amount

of reading and browsing to reach this point, so make it easy to take that next step. You can test design concepts, organization, and content within your marketing automation system to find the optimal look for your landing pages. (We discuss testing in Chapter 16.)

Landing Page Forms

Your landing-page copy is what visitors notice, but your form design can either send your response rates soaring or leave them flat. Form design is the heart of your landing page, so make it easy to find, simple to use, and thorough enough to give you as much vital information as your landing page visitors will share. Once you've put in the work to draw them to your landing page, they must also stay long enough to fill out the form. Ask the right questions and help leads out with answers whenever possible.

What Questions Should Your Landing Page Form Ask?

You only have five or six seconds in which to convince visitors to stay on your landing page, and they'll spend two or three of those seconds looking at your content. That means your form has to be concise and attractive to encourage them to use it. A lengthy form often looks like too much work and contributes to a high bounce rate, but a too-short form misses out on gathering key information. Chapter 8 discussed progressive profiling, and here is where it has its greatest impact. By allowing your AI to keep your forms short and easy to complete, you gain significantly more form completions. Typically, the optimal number of blanks on a form falls between five and 10 blanks, with a high point in the bell-curve distribution around the midpoint. This figure varies by industry, purpose, and a host of other factors, but starting with six or seven blanks and testing to monitor response rates is the best plan of action. Following are six of the most useful pieces of information you can gather from your landing page form. The list isn't exhaustive and you may not need to include them all, but these are the usual inclusions on standard forms.

1. **Name** – This one's a given, but don't forget to include a drop-down menu for titles. Knowing whether you're addressing Mr. Chris Smith, Ms. Chris Smith or Dr. Chris Smith can give you some extra information about your customer. Separating the name field into first and last names is the best practice for easier data maintenance. Your MAI is able to cross-reference information from form to form to ensure clean data both within the system and when synched with your CRM.

2. **Email address** – Aside from your visitors' names, an email address is the most important piece of information you gather. Use reverse appending to derive additional knowledge from this one important data point. You'll also want your prospects' email addresses for future email marketing campaigns.

3. **Phone number** – Although online business and e-commerce are growing rapidly, plenty of business still takes place over the phone. Many landing pages make this blank an optional one, but your form should contain a place for a number even if you don't make it a required field.

4. **Company name** – Almost as important as your prospects' name is the name of company for which they work. You can often infer this information from the domain name of the email address. Use the company name to drill down deeper to see if you've already reached saturation with this client or to explore additional leads within the organization.

5. **Job title** – This information is essential for B2B companies. It will help your AI to generate a BANT profile (see Chapter 5), tailor your content to your audience more precisely, and get a direct line of contact with decision-makers within organizations. Along with your visitors' names and email addresses, it's one field we recommend making mandatory for B2B–oriented landing pages.

6. **URL** – It's not necessary to ask for this information since corporate domains can usually be derived from a B2B prospect's email address. With a site URL, you can surf to the company's website to find a wealth of publicly available information in one convenient place. Look at the About Us or Staff pages, for example, to find other personnel who might also be useful contacts.

Depending on your form, you might also include mailing address, ZIP code, country, number of employees, or any other vital demographics you and your marketing department need to know. Remember, though, that too many spaces to fill leads to a drop-off in participation.

Drop-Down Menus, Radio Buttons, or Blanks?

Some fields are obviously geared to visitor input, but others are best to use as drop-down menus. Drop-down options ensure that you get more accurate results and increase response rates by making life easier on respondents. Income range, job title, number of employees, and dates of birth lend themselves well to a drop-down menu. Because they fold away neatly when not in use, they also look less intimidating on a form than a large field of blanks. Use these menus for lengthy set lists of options, such as the months of the year in a birth date or job titles within an industry.

With employee size and sales volume, it is always better to ask for a range rather than the actual number. It limits errors and makes the data easier to analyze. We also recommend standardizing job function, industry, title, state, and country.

Radio buttons (those little circles or squares that visitors click to select an option from a short list), are often a good choice for smaller data sets. A landing page offering a free T-shirt, for example, might include radio buttons for small, medium, large, and extra-large sizes. Judicious use of radio buttons can streamline forms and vary their visual impact, making them more engaging for visitors to use. With some information, a blank is the only way to go, but use it sparingly to make it easy on your visitors and limit errors. PURLs are the holy grail of forms. A PURL is a personalized landing page that's customized for each individual who reaches his unique destination. Creating these custom forms by hand would be exhausting work, but automation makes it simple. By using a PURL, you're illustrating your customers' importance and making them feel more comfortable with your request, in turn significantly increasing the likelihood of form completion.

In addition to the PURL, you may want to produce an automatically prepopulated form when customers arrive to at their personalized page.

This tactic is ideal for returning visitors and subscribers whose information you have on file from previous orders. Self-populating forms can also make giving postal addresses easier by providing the city and state when the ZIP or ZIP+4 postal codes are typed into the appropriate field. Spare your visitors extra typing and they're more likely to finish the form. But it's also important to have visitors — even returning ones — occasionally fill out blank forms. This way, your Marketing AI can monitor any changes from earlier iterations of the form to the most recent one. If a lead now has a different job title, or changes his postal address, your MAI can update that information in the customer file and alert your sales and marketing teams.

Developing Copy for Your Landing Page

In Chapter 9 we detailed why a great CTA is imperative and how the IOU principle can increase response rates. Those tools are of paramount importance on your landing page because every word counts in such a concentrated format. Using concise headlines, ample white space, bulleted lists, and enticing calls to action keeps your visitors engaged and moves them through your landing page's response form.

Content in Context

Content matters in every aspect of your site, but on your landing page context is also essential. What brought your visitor to the landing page? While a few may happen across it from search engines, almost everyone reaching your landing page does so from clicking a link or directly typing in its URL. To increase conversions and encourage prospects to take the next step of filling in that form, keep the context of what that visitor was doing before he found your website. You'll have all this information available thanks to your Marketing AI, which tracks a given lead's trajectory through your marketing pipeline from the very first visit to your site.

Let's look at an example from a hypothetical email to a subscriber list from a company that develops project-management software for construction companies. The email's offer contains a link to a free white paper on how to choose the right management software package for this competitive sector. The email's call to action, a vivid orange button on a subdued blue background, includes the text "Find Your Software Solution Today." When clicking through, visitors land on a page featuring the same color scheme and an orange button with "Claim Your Software Solution" on it. This campaign and landing page enjoyed an 80 percent higher conversion rate than the previous campaign, which took readers who clicked to a generic template and a yellow "Register Here" button.

Why was there such a difference? Context cues, both visual and textual, linked the initial offer to the landing page and a progressive profiling form that asked only for the individual's name, job function, and email address. They became part of the same conversation, used the same design elements, and included some of the same phrasing. Customers knew they'd found the right place and were instantly reminded why they went to the landing page when they saw the same offer there. They'd already decided that offer was worth a click, so the new site with its matching graphics and text simply confirmed that decision. In addition, limiting the contact information requested on the form reduced the friction to respond.

Attention, Attention!

Your audience's attention on a standard page jumps from place to place to get a clear view of all the information the page contains. When your landing page is optimized, everything they see will point in one direction. Let other pages give an overview of all the benefits and features you can give your customers; your landing page is solely for the specific offer you're making and how it benefits your visitor. You've got her attention, so don't squander it with information she doesn't find relevant right now.

Bulleted lists are popular items for landing pages because they're easy to take in at a glance. People don't typically read them word for word; instead, they take in the information in the bite-size chunks a brief list offers. Keep list elements short and sweet — five or fewer words are enough — and don't overburden the list with too many items. Focus peoples' attention by placing lists above the fold so that viewers take them in as soon as they reach the page.

Images are also excellent ways to capture and direct attention. Simple, bold graphics that illustrate how the product or service you're offering works can be powerful motivators on landing pages. You don't need or want an image-heavy landing page, but graphics that lead to your form (and indicate where visitors should go next) are essential. Your logo should appear prominently on the landing page as well, to ensure visitors who've clicked through know they've reached the right place.

You've learned how your Marketing AI scores leads and orchestrates your omni-channel marketing program to serve those leads the right content at the right time throughout their buying journey. In Chapter 16 you'll see how your Marketing AI uses testing to find out how to make each campaign more effective than the last.

Takeaways:

1. Landing pages must be functional, relevant, targeted, and concise.
2. Your landing page is typically your first-impression destination to new prospects.
3. A successful landing page requests less and produces more.

PART V
ANALYSIS: ACTIONABLE INSIGHTS

CHAPTER 16

TESTING

I f brilliant creative is the art of marketing, then testing is the science. It's the essential ingredient that determines the perfect combination to deliver the right message to the right audience at the right time. Through testing you're able to tune your message to the proper channel, which in turn leads to stronger brand identity, greater relevance, and better customization. When you speak your customers' language, you're more likely to receive a positive response, whether you're asking them to buy or simply convincing them to share their email address or open your email. A/B testing teaches your MAI the vocabulary your prospects "speak." The beauty of multivariate testing is that it continually compares the use of a variety of different data elements to improve your automated system's fluency, making each campaign more effective at achieving your goals than the last.

The average American takes fewer than 10 seconds to decide which of the hundreds of offers they've received each day are worth more of their precious time. With such a deluge of information from other sources and competitors competing for your leads' attention, how do you rise above the noise to get your prospects' attention? There's only one way to know if your message is being received and when the best time to usher leads to a new phase of the Lead Lifecycle is, and that is to test and find out (Chapter 5).

TAFO is the antithesis of guesswork. Some knowledge is counterintuitive, and only rigorous testing can reveal the truth. In this chapter you'll see how your Marketing AI simplifies TAFO and gives you the best possible return on your investments.

Testing Your Way to Higher Response Rates

When you have your eyes examined, you experience one kind of multivariate testing. The ophthalmologist asks you if you can see more clearly with one lens or another, and your answers narrow down other possibilities and targets the optimal range for your vision. A/B (or split) testing uses the same process to bring clarity to your campaigns, focusing on increasingly effective subject lines, content, and other details. Over time, A/B testing hones your marketing strategy to a keen edge, one that that gives you the advantage over your competition.

Marketing relies on guidelines instead of absolute rules; if there were a single, sure-fire way to get a response to every offer everyone would use it, but that isn't how people behave. Audiences differ in what moves them to respond, and what works for one product line may not inspire prospects to take action on another. Through multivariate testing you and your Marketing AI pinpoint the elements that work best for every segment of your audience and optimize your messages to them. By definition, an AI is responsive and capable of learning. A/B testing is how your system understands the realities of the world around it and continually improves the logic needed to respond and thrive in an ever-changing environment.

Multivariate Testing Versus A/B Testing

Statisticians, IT professionals, and marketing experts sometimes use the terms multivariate testing and A/B testing interchangeably, but they aren't the same. A/B testing uses two variables, while multivariate testing can monitor multiple variable responses at once, something your Marketing AI handles with ease.

Multivariate testing changes various aspects of a message, sending slightly different content to a selected audience. For example, one message may contain the "A" phrase "Act now — supplies are limited" as a call to action while another uses the "B" phrase "Call today — sale ends

Saturday." Each of these messages goes out to two different industry segments. The first segment is financial, and the second segment is medical. This set of testing variations results in four test results: 1A, 1B, 2A, and 2B.

When this test is run, it reveals that the financial industry is more supply-conscious and responds better to the A phrase, "supplies are limited." The medical industry is more price-conscious and responds more favorably to the "sale ends Saturday," phrase B. A Marketing AI excels at handling the complexities of multiple variables in a test group and can send the proper message to each segment.

Split testing is a special kind of multivariate testing that uses only two possibilities, an A and a B variant. By keeping other elements of your offer the same and varying only one aspect of the message, your MAI can verify the changes that maximize your desired results. You define successes for your marketing automation system, and once the system ascertains which of two variables more closely approaches that success, it automatically delivers the winning version to the bulk of your audience.

There are many channels you can use to test. Since email is the fastest, least expensive, and most trackable marketing medium, it's an excellent place to begin testing with your audience. Based on the results of your email campaigns, your MAI will deploy your multichannel strategies and launch your lead nurturing strategy to optimize every opportunity. As a result of email marketing's hierarchy on the food chain of lead generation, it's critical to generate maximum results on every email campaign.

Control Versus Challenger

An estimated 70 percent of business email is handled within the first two hours of receipt. That's great news if you want a real-time gauge of the effectiveness of a campaign as it unfolds, and multivariate testing with your MAI is a good way to do that. Using a control-versus-challenger technique, your email undergoes a quick spot-test before it goes out to the total list universe, eliminating risk while increasing the effectiveness of your overall campaign.

Tech teams and creative work together to develop a challenger campaign. The test uses two messages with similar themes, but different details. The A split (also known as the control), is the creative that has proven to generate the most response in the past. The B split (also known as the challenger), contains a new element that you believe will result in better response rates. This method split-tests the message to a small percentage of the global list, usually from 10 to 20 percent. The control version goes to half the test group, and the challenger version is sent to the other half of the test universe. Within a given time period (typically two hours later), the AI determines the version with the best results and automatically sends the winning creative out to the remaining 80 to 90 percent of the list.

Think of it as a kind of competition between your variables. The control variable is the current most-successful result, the reigning champion. As challenger variables rise to battle, it can become the *new* control version if it proves more successful. By using A/B testing, every element in your email or RTP content can become a champion.

Your Marketing AI team can set any number of testing-element metrics to find the best fit for each segment of your marketing database. Open rates, clicks, and other data sets let creative optimize an email for targeting in a wide variety of ways. The automation technology behind multivariate testing can also launch a secondary campaign after the initial communication by using tracking cookies that note when recipients open mail or click through on links. Retargeting is most successful when it's highly focused, and setting trigger conditions can make it even more effective by tailoring with multivariate testing.

Key Email Elements to Test

The number of elements you can test is far greater than even a comprehensive list could name. However, years of testing have shown that the following factors have the greatest influence:

> ➤ **Price** – Other than the email list you use, price can have the greatest overall impact on your results.

➤ **Subject Line** – The first thing your email recipients see, your subject line can be tremendously influential for open rates.

➤ **"From" Name** – Readers use the "from" name on email to screen what they open in the same way they use caller ID to screen phone calls.

➤ **Day of the Week** – You probably don't follow the same routine on a Monday as you do on a Friday, and neither do your prospects. By multivariate testing with mailings, you can find the days on which your audience is most receptive.

➤ **Time of Day** – Do your email messages perform better when your customers see them first thing in the morning, just after lunch or in the evening?

➤ **Frequency** – The right email marketing strategy hits the sweet spot of contacting customers enough to remain in their minds but not enough to be perceived as spam

➤ **Image-Rich versus Text-Rich Mail** – Are your prospects interested in reading your message, or are they primarily visual? Do your products lend themselves to descriptive features or appealing images?

➤ **Short versus Long Copy** – Longer emails aren't always more effective. Some recipients respond best to short, to-the-point messages; others prefer a more detailed explanation of features and benefits.

➤ **Image Size** – For products that have intricate details or plenty of visual appeal, a picture may be worth a thousand words.

➤ **Links versus Buttons** – Buttons are easier to see, but links are embedded within copy that puts them into context. Which is best for your prospects? Test and find out!

➤ **Number of Links** – Ideally, your email should make it as easy as possible for the recipient to take action, and one way to ensure that is to provide plentiful links. Too many links, however, can overwhelm the page and resemble spam, so knowing where to draw the line is key.

➤ **Unsubscribe Message Placement** – Where and how this link appears can influence readers' decisions. We recommend placing the unsubscribe message at the bottom of the page.

> **Subject Line Personalization** – In some industries, placing the recipient's name in the subject line is an eye-catching way to differentiate your message from the rest of in-box contents.

> **Email Body Personalization** – Less controversial than subject line personalization, using a recipient's name in an email salutation is usually the way to go.

> **Animated Gifs** – Movement is instantly eye-catching. With an animated gif, you can showcase a product in use, send a lively message along with your email or make a more lasting impression on anyone who opens your email.

> **Font Colors** – Legibility, brand identity and visual appeal all get a boost when you choose your font colors well.

> **Font Styles** – As with colors, font styles influence readers' perceptions of the message. Clean-lined, sans-serif fonts look crisp for tech and IT industry emails. Times New Roman and traditional serif fonts fit businesses that want to convey stability.

> **Opt-Down Possibilities** – The unsubscribe option doesn't have to be the only action your email recipients can take. With opt-down controls on your preference page, subscribers can choose to throttle the flow of information to a level they find comfortable without having to opt out altogether.

> **Social Sharing Icons** – Where do your email recipients share the information you send them? With multivariate testing of social sharing icons, you can learn how email interacts with the rest of your marketing strategy by including social-sharing icons within the body of or below your message.

> **Social Connection Icons** –A/B testing lets you find out if a button or a link is the best way to encourage forwarding.

> **Delivery by Time Zone** –Email marketers can set email to be delivered at the right moment across any time zone for every member on your email list. For time-sensitive offers, taking time zones into account is especially important.

> **Call to Action Quantity** – For some messages, a single appearance of your call to action may be enough. Other email campaigns do best when they offer multiple opportunities to act or express a single call to action in more than one way.

➢ **Call to Action Placement** – Calls to action most frequently appear near the end of your email copy, but many have found better success placing the CTA at the top of the page.

➢ **Social Proof** – Build positive publicity about your products and services, and you've won a major victory over your competition. When you use social proof in your emails via testimonials, links to glowing press releases or awards you've won, you give your readers a reason to sit up and take notice.

Testing in Other Channels

When your email readers respond, where do they land? A/B testing is invaluable for assessing the effectiveness of landing pages. Depending on your site layout, your intended audience, and the specific subject of your campaign, your landing pages may look markedly different from each other. Unlike other pages on your site, landing pages are calibrated to work with a particular offer and call to action, giving you far greater control over the testing process. Monitoring the complex interactions between customer behavior and personalized landing pages is too big a job for a human marketer, but AI-assisted real-time personalization automates the process. Using your MAI to test site content gives you results quickly, allowing the system to adjust on the fly.

Many of the elements we've listed as important for email testing also work with landing pages, including CTA placement, social media attribution, design palette, and content, all of which are simple to change from a marketing automation dashboard. Forms are another aspect of landing pages that lend themselves well to split testing. Try one with radio buttons and another with a drop-down menu for the same information to find which format your audience prefers. You can also test the number of fields you list, the information you request, or the images you use to encourage your audience to complete the process.

Telemarketing and testing also go together well. Because each call is structured and follows a set flow, you can test elements like prospects' first or last name, time of day, length of call, and order in which the information is presented. The key to using A/B testing in telemarketing campaigns is consistency; your marketing personnel must stick to the format closely to get relevant, accurate test results and to improve your next campaign. Here's where your Marketing AI shines yet again, as it collects data in the background and compiles it into easily actionable analytics.

Testing Your Brand

It's often useful to investigate how your brand is perceived, and split variable testing can provide deep insight into your brand identity. Surveys are useful, too, as they can tell you what is important to your prospects and customers, where they intend to allocate their budgets, and the reasoning behind their marketing direction.

What leads tell you about your brand is only part of the story, as we've discussed (see Chapter 4). Behavioral and contextual data tells you more about how leads are really interacting with you across multiple channels. Your Marketing AI shows you what works best to build your brand and to enhance engagement across all channels and within each platform.

When you release content to your audience, is it perceived as sage advice from an industry expert, an authoritative statement from a trusted source, or a message from a friend? The tone of your content matters more than you think when communicating with your clientele, and through A/B testing you can find just the right tenor with which to connect to each segment of your audience.

Some industries naturally lend themselves to a third-person, informative tone, while others are conducive to a chatty, second-person voice. See how your prospects respond when you send a message that comes from a slightly different angle than your usual tone, and you may be surprised at how much of a difference it makes to giving your brand greater authority or becoming friendlier with your potential customers.

A/B Testing Tips

> ➢ Although you can change multiple variables at once, any scientist will tell you that doing so can create confounding factors. To isolate and assess the effectiveness of changes in your email

campaigns, limiting your number of variables produces the clearest results.

➢ Know what you and your marketing team are testing. Some changes affect open rates or social sharing; others affect click-throughs and sales.

➢ Monitoring is vital to the success of A/B testing. The MAI's ability to learn is predicated on letting your audience vote with their responses to choose their preference, so analysis after the fact is essential. You have incredibly powerful tools available to you from the moment you install your MAS, but installation is not the same as implementation. The adaptive, responsive technology and knowledgeable personnel to collect and interpret the data your tests accumulate are both critical elements of success.

➢ Keep an open mind during the testing process. You may be surprised to find that your audience responds positively to image-rich, colorful emails or that your best customers do their shopping in the wee hours of the morning. Remember, TAFO is the only way to get real answers; assumptions are only guesswork.

Real-Time Personalization Using Test Results

Here's why testing matters so much: With it, you're able to meet leads' needs in real-time, which in turn dramatically increases their velocity through your sales funnel. Your Marketing AI delivers the content they want to see when they want to see it, reducing friction as they move through the pipeline to sales readiness. Testing is essential to the process because it determines what's optimal for your audience so your MAI can deliver customized information to them.

We introduced RTP in Chapter 8. Now let's look at three elements of real-time personalization in order:

➢ **Dynamic:** Outmoded landing pages, banner ads, and corporate sites present the same information that becomes stale to returning visitors, but your MAI uses dynamic RTP to fit the needs of whoever's viewing the page. By changing out generic, static landing-page content in favor of ever-changing, responsive forms and content that adapt to your prospect's Lead Lifecycle based on the information the MAI collects on visitors, companies can multiply response rates immediately.

➢ **Creative:** Change for change's sake is irrelevant. Your results will improve as your creative keeps pace with the stage the lead has reached. Your audience responds best when you feed them the content they're searching for at each Lead Lifecycle stage, creating a synergy between your MAI and your audience.

➢ **Optimized:** What makes one piece of content better than another? How closely it matches your audience's needs is what matters most, and discovering that happens only with testing. To get optimal results, your Marketing AI needs to be able to identify the elements, including copy, offer, timing, design, and channel, that best resonate with your audience.

Using RTP, your MAI immediately increases the quality of leads flowing into your marketing pipeline, because it's already delivering the kind of information that most closely aligns with prospect's Lead Lifecycle stage. Here's a quick look at two B2B examples (see Chapter 12 for SEO keyword tips):

Example 1.: Jack and Jill
Jack and Jill are prospects searching for a training program that can help their company's sales team close more leads. They each do a Google search for the words *sales training* and click on a listing in the search engine's results page.

The landing page Jack is taken to immediately serves up an offer for a report titled "The 7 Most Important Things to Consider When Choosing a Sales Training Program." When Jack clicks on the offer and submits his contact information, he enters the sales training lead-nurture track. Instead of being offered a report, Jill is taken to a landing page offering a free, no-obligation consultation with a sales training expert.

The short-tail keyword *sales training* that both Jack and Jill used indicates that they're at the beginning of the Lead Lifecycle, a determination that is confirmed by the AI's analysis of the results. The report offer and follow-up nurture stream Jack took have proven to be three times more likely to enter the pipeline as a sales qualified lead than the consultation offer made to Jill.

Example 2.: Alicia and Ted

Alicia and Ted are also searching for a training program for their sales team. They do a Google search for the long-tail keywords *sale-training program closest to me*. Alicia is greeted with an offer to have a free, no-obligation consultation with a sales training expert, and Ted gets the "The 7 Most Important Things to Consider When Choosing a Sales Training Program" report offer.

This time, though, the results are quite different. The long-tail keywords indicate that these leads are in the advanced stage of the Lead Lifecycle. They're ready to buy, and this fact is confirmed by the AI's analysis of the results. Here, the offer of a free consultation has proven to be three times more likely to convert than the report, which is appropriate to a middle-of-funnel lead.

As a result of these tests, future leads are served the proper content based on the keyword searched. Thanks to RTP, future leads will now get the most relevant content and maximize conversions. To uncover which channel and program contributed to the sale, you need to go a step farther by delving into attribution, and that's where we're headed in Chapter 17.

Takeaways:

1. Always subscribe to the rule of TAFO — Test And Find Out
2. A/B testing uses two variables while multivariate testing can utilize multiple variables at once.
3. Don't just test in one channel; apply tests to every marketing channel and campaign.

CHAPTER 17

ATTRIBUTION

Attribution is the process by which you trace the pathways and apply the proper costs and the revenue received by each lead that enters your database. It tracks all the channels, programs, campaigns, and touchpoints your leads use to become customers and allows you to truly understand the cost benefit relationships of each.

Attribution has changed dramatically with the rise of digital marketing. In the old world of marketing, when marketers only reached their customers via direct mail, telemarketing, and newspaper print ads, analyzing the value of each of these channels was a manual (and often impossible) job.

Although marketing has grown increasingly complex, testing out which digital-marketing channels give you the greatest return on your investment is far more accurate and complete in the 21st century. It is the key to making your marketing scalable, predictable, reliable, and sustainable.

In this chapter we detail how to properly track attribution, get accurate data about your real traffic sources, and gain insight into the value each channel contributes to your company's revenue.

Why Attribution Matters

You may see the last click a potential customer made to reach your landing page, but that action is only the final one in a string of other impressions and transactions that led your prospect to seek you out and choose you over your competitors. Understanding attribution marketing is more important than ever because the data behind it is the key to making your company more successful.

How your prospects arrive at a buying decision is a process, not a one-time choice. They might have a need and actively search for the product through Google searches, crowd-sourced review sites, social media, and articles. Conversely, they might not realize that they need what you sell until they see an ad for it, receive a direct mail piece, or an email promotion. The buyer's journey in B2B industries is complex. Attribution tracks every successful interaction that resulted in the lead becoming a customer. Below are two important ideas about what it means to your bottom line when attribution follows prospects through their whole journey, not just one step.

1. You're better able to plan your budget across multiple channels. Knowing your ROI on each aspect of your marketing strategy lets your Marketing AI allocate resources where they matter most. You learn how digital channels interact to form a whole that's greater than the sum of its parts. When your MAI discovers what combination of channels generated your best customers, and the true costs associated with each, you can improve your marketing effectiveness by applying the right leverage to these key areas identified by your attribution tools.

2. You gain more insight into your audience. You already know it's critical to build a strong, detailed customer profile to expand your market reach and enjoy higher retention rates. Attribution plays an important role in giving you a better, more accurate picture of your audience data. Your Marketing AI integrates your marketing in digital and offline formats seamlessly. Your prospects and customers typically come to know you through multiple channels, and with proper attribution, you find out what those channels are and how you can optimize them.

Attribution Marketing Theory

When prospects reach your landing pages, you can readily check their previous stop. Did they click through a link in an email or newsletter?

Was your most recent blog post or direct mail piece the trigger? Did they find you via a banner ad, Facebook post, a Google search, or a tweet? Knowing the last source is important, but it doesn't tell the whole story. That last click credit could be attributing greater success to a particular marketing channel while underestimating the value of another that's performing exceptionally at an earlier point in the attribution chain.

We discussed in Chapter 2 how both branding and the importance of familiarity are important. Attribution marketing using a Marketing AI quantifies that familiarity and assigns weight not only to that single-source attribution data you find on a Google Analytics report, but also to the steps that led to that point. For example, single-source attribution tells you that you acquired a prospect from your PPC campaign. More sophisticated attribution models drill deeper into all the channels that influenced that prospect on his way to becoming your customer. Was he clicking on your company's newsletter? Did your lead also respond to an email offering a whitepaper? Along the way to becoming a customer, did that prospect also meet with your sales staff at a tradeshow?

Tracking prospects' behavior becomes more difficult as you move farther back along the attribution chain, unless you have an AI that can store such complex information in its database. Having hard data and accurate analytics make sophisticated attribution models valuable as predictive tools. The specific algorithms behind them aren't within this book's scope, but it's useful to get a glimpse of how attribution theory is put into practice to produce real-world results. Models fall into a few general groups:

Single-Source Attribution
You're already familiar with these simple models (Figure 17.1). They randomly assign all the weight to one part of the attribution chain. The most common attribution tools, including traffic counts and source listings in your onsite analytics, give all the attribution credit to the last site a prospect visited. Many companies are simply unable to track customer contact. In this model, the companies are unaware of the successful interactions that influenced the sale, so they assign all the credit to the salesperson.

First-Touch Attribution

First-touch attribution (FTA) has great value. It tracks leads from all of your marketing channels and reports on how *new* qualified leads were first produced along with the revenue they produce and their associated marketing costs. This model gives all the weight to the campaign and channel from which the lead was first added to the database.

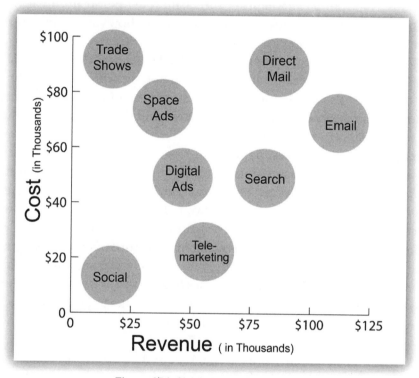

Figure 17.1: Single-Touch Attribution

What you learn from FTA are important criteria to measure because if not for the channel or campaign that created the success, you would not have generated a new customer. These analytics are also useful for spotting problem areas. Your AI will alert you if traffic falls precipitously from a once-productive channel. You'll know something has gone wrong from that source. An incorrect link, a misplaced banner ad, a drop in keyword rank, or an email that didn't reach its target audience is easy to find when you look at a single-source attribution report.

Multi-touch Attribution

A more sophisticated way to distribute revenue attribution is to apply a multi-touch model (Figure 17.2). These models have great analytic value as they give credit to the multiple channels used to affect the decision to buy. Multi-touch attribution is made possible by MASs capable of tracking leads from first touch to the moment they become customers. These systems assign *fractional* weight to successful touchpoints in the attribution chain, and create a more detailed picture of how your prospects are converted into customers.

Some multi-touch models assign equal value to every successful interaction on the attribution ladder, while others give more weight at certain steps. The single most important element of a successful multi-touch attribution model is the ability to define the terms of each success. A success is reached when the prospect takes an action that shows engagement with your company.

For example, although opening an email may show enough interest to add to the behavior score, it takes a click through to show engagement. Therefore, only emails that have received clicks have shown the success necessary to get multi-touch attribution. Different channels have different definitions of success: For example, a customer who has signed up for a webinar must have attended, and a customer attending a tradeshow must have engaged with your sales team at your booth to qualify as a successful result. Your MAI tracks all successes, allocating proper credit and cost to the activity that produced the result.

The results look like this (Figure 17.2):

Both single and multi-touch models have their advantages and both should be used. The following example using "ABC Company" illustrates how multi-touch analytics provides insight into the contributions that sales and marketing each make to the company's success:

ABC Company specializes in financial software. It has adopted a plan to improve its analytics by using marketing automation. To broaden awareness, the firm has exhibited at a trade show, created a new client-testimonial video linked to its website, and sent out brochures to segmented markets via direct mail. Its

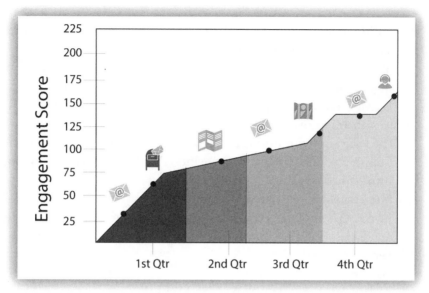

Figure 17.2: Multi-touch Attribution

single-touch attribution shows a significant jump in traffic credited to the trade show, but its multi-touch analysis shows that a substantial number of prospects converted to customers after clicking on an email linked to the client-testimonial video.

The result: Marketing gained a great deal of respect from the sales manager for creating the email and the video. Without the AI's multi-touch attribution model, the sales manager would not have understood the role that marketing played in increasing the company's sales, and marketing would not have been able to properly allocate its budget where the investment matters most.

The Mechanics of Attribution in a Marketing AI

The concepts and math behind attribution models are fairly simple. But the mechanics of retaining clear, concise, accurate data for attribution is where your Marketing AI really shines. Whether your data comes from your CRM system or your MAS, the attribution still depends on your marketing channel and your campaign approach. Following are seven data sources your Marketing AI typically uses to build detailed source attribution:

1. **CRM** – Synced lead from the CRM. It's important to code these as a Sales Captured Lead
2. **MAS** – Synced lead from the Marketing Automation System. It's important to code these as a Marketing Captured Lead
3. **Email cookies** – Tracking cookies embedded in emails feed a wealth of information back to your AI. This method is key to tracking anonymous visitor activity so you can record behavior before the lead registers, provides their email address or logs into your system.
4. **Site tracking cookies** – Like cookies attached to email, JavaScript and site tracking cookies can trace how users interact with your site, including recording data about how they reached you.
5. **Pass parameters** – Most browsers, including those on smartphones and tablets pass a digital trail that can tell your AI how the lead found their way to you.
6. **PURLs** – Personal URLs are great at connecting offline advertising with your AI.
7. **Visitor or customer surveys** – Sometimes the best way to learn how your visitors discovered you is to ask them. "How did you hear about us?" is a standard question in customer surveys, because it's critical to finding your most successful and relevant marketing channels.

Five Questions Your Attribution Analytics Should Answer

Looking past primary sources to find secondary and tertiary attributions is vital to omni-channel marketing, but what can it do specifically, and how much of a difference does it make to your bottom line?

1. **How does the Marketing AI's model measure each channel's performance?** In single-source attribution data the answer is straightforward, because it puts all the weight on one step of the process. Single-source models are great for getting an overview and remain a cornerstone of any analysis dashboard. Fractional attribution models are designed to give you a view that helps you

understand the interrelationship between sales and marketing channels, optimizing your return on your multichannel marketing investment.

2. **How does attribution describe the actual value of each marketing channel?** Your MAI's attribution-marketing strategy alerts you to potential growth areas, identifies underperforming channels, and integrates your data for more effective campaigns in the future. With responsive, effective attribution models, you see where your leads originate, receive alerts when problems occur, and gain key insight into how each channel relates to others, an important factor when deciding where to focus your attention.

3. **How can this attribution model make ROI more readily measurable?** Tracking multichannel contact by hand is impossibly complex, but AI is made for crunching big numbers and building a simple picture from big data.

4. **How will attribution reveal the interrelationship of channels?** Attribution is a chain of events. Every move your prospects take to find you is a link in that chain, a buy signal to you that may remain hidden without a Marketing AI's attribution analytics. By seeing how one channel leads directly or indirectly to others, your MAI develops insight into how each aspect of your omni-channel marketing campaign depends on others. Seeing these interrelationships can help you develop force multipliers for future campaigns; by bumping up the volume on the most influential channels, you increase interest in the channels that depend on it. It is also an essential part of creating a marketing program that is scalable, predictable, reliable, and can be sustained over time.

5. **How can a Marketing AI's attribution model show where to make cuts?** The flip side of seeing how to bring more force to bear by amplifying key channels within your overall marketing strategy is to know where you can dial back your efforts. You can have confidence in your decisions when you have a multi-touch analysis that identifies the channels that have little impact on customer acquisition.

Comprehensive Attribution

Currently, even those companies that track attribution may not be putting the whole picture into perspective because they monitor data for online and offline channels separately. Being able to quantify the effect direct mail or telemarketing can have on digital activity is crucial to improving ROI across all channels. There's no one-size-fits-all approach to comprehensive attribution models, but the industry's moving in that direction. It's important to recognize that your audience is consuming content through multiple media and through multiple devices. Proper attribution will help illustrate the clearest engagement picture.

As important as attribution data is on its own, it becomes even more valuable when put in a format that lets you make full use of it. In Chapter 18, we discuss what it takes to create a dynamic analysis dashboard that puts all your data in one place and maximizes its utility.

Takeaways:

1. Attribution tracks all channels, programs, campaigns, and touchpoints your lead uses to become a customer.
2. First touch, last touch, and every touch are the most common attribution models.
3. Online and offline channels need to factor into your attribution model.

CHAPTER 18

ANALYTICS AND DASHBOARDS

No system is better equipped to perform in-depth analysis of your marketing plan, both in real-time and in looking back at historical data, than a Marketing AI. It tracks behavioral data and contextualizes it as it happens, so your MAI lets you analyze the impact of different marketing elements over a period of time. It learns and advances your programs in response to your customers' actions and your marketing team's input. When you're able to identify how people move through the Lead Lifecycle, you can run multivariate tests to find the best possible course of action, gaining valuable information for dashboards that let you check your marketing campaign's health at a glance. Your AI reduces friction and streamlines marketing flows to make the journey even easier for your prospects. It also lets you look ahead, improving predictive success with each campaign's analytics. Think of it as your marketing strategy's past, present, and future in one concise package.

Analytics without an effective dashboard to organize information into a usable format is like a library with no system to tell you where to find the specific books you need. Knowledge is power — but only if you know where to find it. A Marketing AI not only amasses information and derives knowledge from it but it builds a dashboard to make that knowledge accessible to users.

The dashboard of your car is designed to let you make rapid decisions without forcing you to take your eyes off the road. Based on frequent, at-a-glance analysis of your speedometer, fuel gauge, engine temperature, and other details, you know instantly when it's time to accelerate or if you need to economize on fuel until you reach the next filling station. Your MAI's dashboard serves the same function, giving you actionable insights that decisively assess your marketing campaign's success based on a set of easily accessible KPIs.

Having a visual display of pertinent information and KPIs lets you measure your campaign against your goals, communicate your successes and challenges to others, and improve each successive campaign based on sound data analysis. With a well-designed dashboard, you can intuit larger trends and interconnections within your data just by looking at a single graph or noting traffic volume changes.

With your MAI you aren't limited to a single dashboard. Your AI team can create nested dashboards that give you a more in-depth look at each channel within your campaign, taking you from the overview dash to modular displays (just as your car shows your trip odometer and overall mileage at the press of a button). You might also find it useful to develop different displays for other departments. With customized dashboard design, you can show your finance department important budget and cost information, give your content-creation team insight into keyword relevance, and show the C-level team how your marketing acumen is paying off.

The point of a dashboard is to make knowledge accessible, not to bury vital statistics under an avalanche of data. You have an AI expressly to handle big data; let your MAI do its job and put the key information it learns in a clear dashboard format for you. When you develop a dashboard that gives you just the right amount of information and presents it in a format that streamlines decision-making, you make that information actionable.

Building a Better Marketing Analytics Dashboard

Whether you choose a custom-built dashboard or work with an out-of-box product that allows you to adjust your display and reflect just the knowledge you need, you first have to decide what goes on it. Data has a habit of clamoring for your attention — everything feels important. But if you included everything on your dashboard, it would no longer serve its purpose. To cut through the clutter and develop a concise, action-able-insight dashboard, answer the following questions:

1. Who is the intended audience? An internal dashboard created expressly for marketing analysis will have greater detail and more technical terminology than one intended for an interdepartmental dashboard. External dashboards meant for C-level executives are likewise lighter on technical jargon and heavier on graphs and bars. Before figuring out what your dashboard needs to say, consider the audience you're addressing.

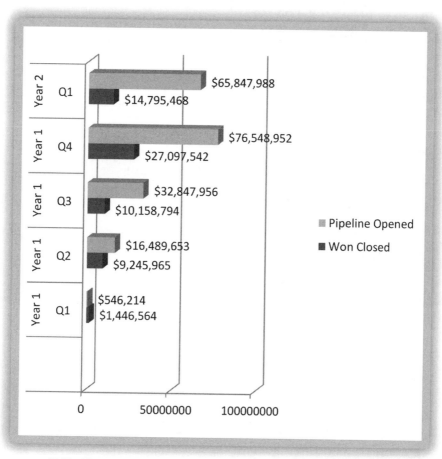

Table 18.1: Opportunities Created vs. Opportunities Won Analysis

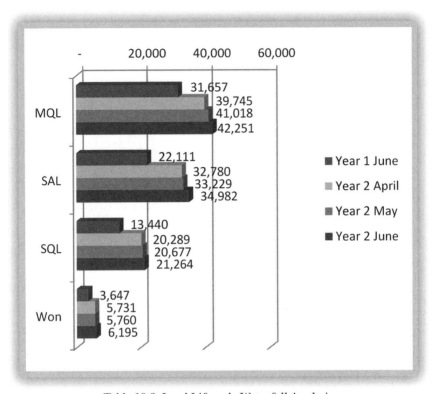

Table 18.2: Lead Lifecycle Waterfall Analysis

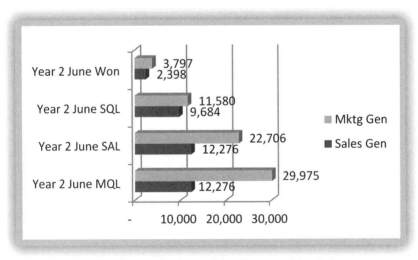

Table 18.3: Marketing vs Sales Generated Analysis

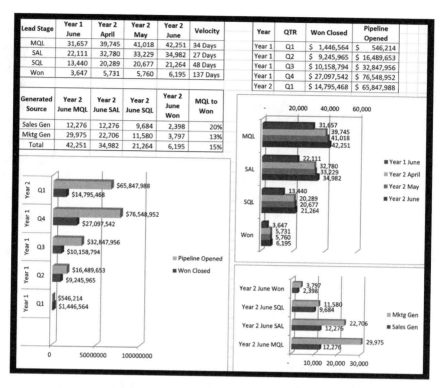

Lead Stage	Year 1 June	Year 2 April	Year 2 May	Year 2 June	Velocity
MQL	31,657	39,745	41,018	42,251	34 Days
SAL	22,111	32,780	33,229	34,982	27 Days
SQL	13,440	20,289	20,677	21,264	48 Days
Won	3,647	5,731	5,760	6,195	137 Days

Year	QTR	Won Closed	Pipeline Opened
Year 1	Q1	$ 1,446,564	$ 546,214
Year 1	Q2	$ 9,245,965	$ 16,489,653
Year 1	Q3	$ 10,158,794	$ 32,847,956
Year 1	Q4	$ 27,097,542	$ 76,548,952
Year 2	Q1	$ 14,795,468	$ 65,847,988

Generated Source	Year 2 June MQL	Year 2 June SAL	Year 2 June SQL	Year 2 June Won	MQL to Won
Sales Gen	12,276	12,276	9,684	2,398	20%
Mktg Gen	29,975	22,706	11,580	3,797	13%
Total	42,251	34,982	21,264	6,195	15%

Table 18.4: Marketing AI Lead Lifecycle Analytics Dashboard

2. What do you really need — not just want — to know? Some dashboard items are a given. Just as your car needs a speedometer, your website dashboard needs a traffic indicator, for example. You need to know how many new leads have entered your pipeline, how those leads are progressing to opportunities, and how many became customers. Other details are a tougher call. Do you need to know detailed traffic metrics from past campaigns, or is it enough for a given dashboard to illustrate overall proportions with a bar graph? Are your cost-per-lead analytics represented monthly, quarterly, by channel, in dollars, on a graph, or in numbers on a table? Again, the answers here depend on your audience.

3. What are your KPIs? They are linked to revenue goals, pipeline opened and pipeline closed, and won. Sometimes they represent a direct relationship, such as when an increase in qualified leads means an increase in revenue. At other times they represent an inverse relationship; decreasing bounce rates, for example, mean an increase in engagement. In many cases KPIs are derived from other data instead of raw figures. For example, it's useful to know both open and click rates for your email marketing campaigns, but the ratio of clicks to total opens is a more important indicator of engagement than either data set alone. You would want to include this click-to-open rate (CTOR) in your engagement dashboard.

4. How frequently will your MAI update the dashboard information? Some data-driven dashboards update in real-time, on the quarter-hour, or on the hour. They're particularly useful for volatile data that changes rapidly. Others are designed to update daily, weekly, or monthly. Your time scale will determine what goes on your dashboard because some elements show very little change over shorter intervals.

5. How will your dashboard express data? The human eye naturally loves variety. Use that innate trait to make your analysis dashboard design compelling and easy to read. Use a combination of text, bar graphs, line graphs, needle gauges, and other graphical elements whenever possible to illustrate concepts effectively and communicate quickly.

6. How does your dashboard fit with the overall flow of leads through your marketing funnel? Like so many other aspects of your Marketing AI's architecture, the Lead Lifecycle governs many of your dashboard layouts. Analytics that relate to lead scoring, sales readiness, costs per lead, and alerts sent to sales show you the number and velocity of leads moving through your sales funnel. Figure 18.1 is an illustration of the dollar amount of sales closed versus the projected opportunities expected to convert into sales.

Capturing Social Media Data for Analytics

Tracking social media information has historically been a challenge. Fortunately, a Marketing AI is an outstanding data-capture tool that not only links information across social media channels, but also throughout a lead's history. Users who register for newsletters, webinars, or other events via social media channels indicate good interest, so any social media dashboard should include this information. Additional key social metrics include:

1. The number of people in total network: Watching this figure increase or decrease tells you volumes about the health of your social media reach.
2. The number of referred visitors: Spot your brand ambassadors by seeing who refers others to your sites via retweeting and forwarding messages.

Time Is Money: Defining Your Marketing Success Dashboard

After asking a few vital questions about the purpose of the dashboard, think in broad terms about the information it needs to contain. Generally, these boil down to three elements: time, money, and goals.

Time

Your analysis dashboard is your marketing odometer; it doesn't only measure where you are, but also where you've been and where you're headed. Just as important, your dashboard also measures how quickly you're getting there, and knowing your speed is critical to success. Whether as a comparison of former data or as a measure of velocity, time is an essential dimension for most dashboards, which is one reason why line graphs are such a popular feature. When tracking progress over time, they offer a concise, easily read visual to tell your audience about trends. Depending on what you're tracking, you might also find adjustable time intervals useful. Seeing site traffic details for the past hour may not show you much, but looking at a week's worth of visits could reveal important trends. With your MAI, you can automatically generate reports or select custom intervals to gain the best perspective on your analytics.

Money

In Chapter 17 we discussed the importance of accurate attribution to determine marketing dollars spent. Your dashboard helps you track spending and conversions, volume per sale, and other KPIs. Depending on the purpose of your dashboard and its intended audience, the financial aspects may be front and center or take a back seat to other details, but they'll almost always be a part of a general overview dashboard.

Goals

Illustrating change over time and monitoring profitability are critical to defining your goals and how well your campaign achieves them. Needle gauges, vertical bars, and other visual representations work well to depict goals at a glance. Automatically generated reports your MAS produces include dashboards for sales readiness, lead generation, marketing flow monitoring, and omni-channel traffic data.

KPIs

Every channel through which you market is a two-way street that feeds data back to your Marketing AI, teaching it new information with every outgoing campaign. Direct mail, email, PPC, SEO, site analytics, and telemarketing are rich mines of information, and a well-designed dashboard makes that data instantly usable. Digital data culled from email, social media, and website information may be easier to track than other metrics, but all are key performance indicators that should be used in developing an effective dashboard.

A compact dashboard probably won't include all KPIs, but from the ones that are included you and your marketing team can readily assemble a sleek, effective dashboard that does everything you ask of it.

Total Traffic

No analysis is complete without data about your entire audience. How many people visit your website, engage with your social media channels, or open and read your emails and blog in a day? How about in a week or a month? If these figures are low, your MAI will show it and your dashboard can point you toward expanding your reach. If you have plenty of traffic but low engagement, that also tells a story — one you want to rewrite with more relevant content for a happier ending. Your overall traffic is key information from which other data is derived, so it's a prominent feature of your dashboard even when hidden within other data.

Traffic Sources

Here's where attribution comes to the fore. Knowing your most important traffic sources tells your marketing team where to focus its attention and lets your MAI shift resources to where they're most effective.

Lead Lifecycle

The quantity of leads in each stage: monthly, quarterly and year over year indicate the overall health of your sales and marketing program. It also alerts you if leads are getting stuck in any of these stages:

- ✓ Anonymous
- ✓ New (Sales or Marketing Captured Lead)
- ✓ Marketing Engaged
- ✓ MQL
- ✓ SQL
- ✓ Won
- ✓ Lost
- ✓ Recycled
- ✓ Not a lead/Junk

Program Performance

- ✓ First Touch Attribution: This report shows the costs and revenue generated by each program
- ✓ Program Performance Multi-Touch Attribution: This report shows the shared costs and revenues generated by each channel.
- ✓ Omni-channel Opportunity Analysis: This report shows the channels that influenced the lead's conversion to a customer.
- ✓ Success Path Analysis: This report identifies the influence of the sales and marketing team in the lead's conversion to a customer. It indicates how closely sales and marketing are working in tandem.

ROI

Understanding how your investments pay off, whether across multiple marketing channels or within a single one over time, is imperative to revenue marketing. Your MAI tracks your returns on investments and lets your marketing team take action on that knowledge via your dashboard to see where you get the most value. Recall from Chapter 17 the impact your attribution marketing has on ROI; it's here that your MAI incorporates attribution information into tracking cost-per-lead, overall revenue, and other KPIs that reveal your return on investments.

Repeat Customers

Customer retention is vital to your organization's long-term health. By noting which email addresses regularly open and click through, which visitors return to your website, and which social media followers interact with you, your AI constructs a clear image of your most attentive, engaged customers. Depending on your industry, the top 20 percent of your customers probably accounts for about 80 percent of your sales, so use your analytics dashboard to identify these highly engaged customers and keep them satisfied.

Email Open Rate

Open rates are your most basic email metric, and by looking at who's doing the opening, you get a clearer picture of your most interested prospects. Your MAI can look at open rates, cross-reference them with the other data you have on file, and generate a beautifully segmented view of who's most interested in what you have to say. Slicing industry sectors into smaller market segments may reveal that while one company type's sales seem flat, *you* are experiencing great sales volume with one subgroup and a sharp drop in another. Seeing this information on your dashboard will help you refocus your efforts on upward trends while you take a closer look at plateaus to determine their underlying causes. Your open rates are also a great indication of your deliverability into your customer's inboxes, and fluctuations should be closely monitored.

Click Rate

Whether in email, on banner ads, or in SEO content, your click rate provides prime data for analysts. Each click is a vote of confidence, and by overlaying click rates with other information, you build a clearer picture of your prospects for future campaigns. These figures can vary wildly from sector to sector, so what looks like a lukewarm result in one channel might be spectacular performance for another. Usually, acquisition click rates like those from banner ads are low, ranging from 0.2 to 2 percent on average. Retention click rates average closer to 4 percent.

It's helpful to break click rate into market segments for ready analysis. Bar and linear graphs sometimes reveal peaks of interest among some subsets of your universal audience. Knowing where that peak of interest lies on a graph of your customer base and its click rate lets your data team dig deeper and uncover why that group finds your blog, website or email offer particularly compelling.

Click-to-Open Ratio

We touched on the importance of CTORs as a KPI, but they merit a closer look. Once you know your email open rate and click rate, your MAI instantly calculates the click-to-open ratio, a derived measurement that expresses overall interest in a single elegant number. Sometimes called the effective rate, your CTOR gives you a way to measure interest directly. It adds another dimension of knowledge to the base click rates and open rates an email campaign generates. CTORs range from 10 to 30 percent on average, but seeing spikes of 35 percent or more in some sectors is a clear sign that your ideal customer lives in that market segment.

Bounce Rate

Search engines closely track bounce rates, and so should your MAI's site-analytics dashboard. Like CTOR, bounce rate is another prime indicator of engagement; if visitors don't stay on your site long, it's probably because they aren't finding what they expected to find. Sometimes that's because a site is short on relevant content, which is why search engines consider a low bounce rate a signal of quality. Even if your site is free of keyword-stuffed or thin content, your organic search results and site traffic could benefit from a lower bounce rate. By monitoring this metric, you can help your audience's expectations and your offers to align more closely, ensuring greater relevance and keep bounce rates low.

Keyword Analysis

Keywords play a pivotal role in traffic from search engines, and it's critical to track how your target keywords perform. Through regular analysis of your keyword performance, your Marketing AI spots market trends so you can catch rising waves in your industry before they crest.

Offer Results

Offer results depend on the nature of your campaign. Often, it's simply a measure of conversions or sales, but this data can also refer to subscription rates, responses, or survey participants. No matter what kind of offer you make, one principle holds true: The higher the response rate, the better. Your data team should look for those all-important peaks in offer response rates when compared against other aggregate data. You might find your best response rates come from unexpected sources. Off-label uses of your products can become valuable new markets, but only if you identify that vanguard of customers who saw your product or service in a new light.

Site Penetration

The "site" in this metric isn't your website but your prospects' workplaces. Typically used in B2B marketing, site-penetration metrics measure how deeply your marketing efforts reach into an organization. That's critical to know when you're trying to reach the decision makers within the company or want to know when you've reached saturation. To measure site penetration, you need a wealth of historical data about your visitors, and for that you need the power of marketing automation. Your data-discovery process shows whether you're getting the maximum revenue for your marketing spend with each company. Forms, data appends, anonymous browser cookies and other AI-assisted means will contribute vital information to your site-penetration analytics.

There could be a good reason for low site penetration: If the industry you're dealing with isn't an appropriate target market, for example, you might not make much headway. Low penetration may tell you there just isn't much need for your product and lets you cut your losses. The companies that do need your product, though, represent a significant place for increased spend in target industries. Use this report to locate companies you should retarget heavily and which ones you should phase out of your marketing efforts.

If your database contains one executive in a company with 1,000 employees, for example, you aren't getting the site penetration you need to gain a significant percentage of the opportunity that company represents. By using reliable data append and good list hygiene, you reveal your true level of site penetration and can include it on your dashboard.

This key indicator can also advise when you should shut off a particular site if you've recorded no response from it.

Opt-Outs

Since your email database is your most precious asset (see Chapter 9), we don't need to speak at length about the importance of maintaining a large and vibrantly healthy one. Attrition is an inevitable part of marketing life, but it should be closely monitored. Any spike in your opt-out rates should be investigated and remedied immediately. All the measures you take to increase your email reach will be for naught if more records are opting out than allowing permission in.

How Big Should Your Dashboard Be?

While there's no absolute answer for how much information your dashboard should include, think about how car dashboards are designed. They usually contain no more than five or six visible gauges. They may have other information placed low on a center console, as part of a heads-up display, or on an accessory like a GPS navigator, but they don't put those details front and center, where they might distract a driver. Pride of place is reserved for the fuel readout, speedometer, and oil temperature — the KPIs of your car.

In general your Marketing AI's displays should follow the same structure and confine your dashboard to four to six key pieces of information. For example, an email marketing–analysis dashboard that focuses on ROI might include a segmented breakdown of open rates, click-to-open ratio, conversion rates, a graph of the three previous campaigns' open rates, and price per sale. For more detailed analyses, nest other details within broader categories on your main dashboard for simplicity's sake.

The data you've collected and organized in an analysis dashboard forms the basis for a new round of discovery, provides actionable insights, and brings your marketing full circle. You've seen how the discovery and execution phases work; in Part IV we take a look at

our friends at SEO Schematics in a start-to-finish case study of its
Marketing AI implementation.

Takeaways:

1. Develop your dashboard around your KPIs.
2. Don't try to fit every key metric into one dashboard.
3. Accurately identifying ROI is critical for every organization.

Part VI

Case Study: SEO Schematics

THE SEO SCHEMATICS CASE STUDY

Throughout *Marketing AI: From Automation to Revenue Performance Marketing*, we refer to SEO Schematics, a fictitious company that we use to present examples of particular marketing automation challenges and successes. Now we present a case study, also based on our fantasy firm, and unveil how the company adopted a cohesive Lead Lifecycle and incorporated automation into its marketing department, and in the process transformed its entire revenue-marketing strategy.

Company and Product Description: SEO Schematics creates software to monitor search-engine rankings and improve optimization. The company builds affordable, easy-to-use tools to track and improve organizations' SEO rankings, social marketing engagement, and link building.

Marketing Challenge: SEO Schematics hit a critical snag in its growth cycle. Its marketing consisted primarily of direct mail, email, SEO, SMO, and trade shows, but these channels weren't effectively producing the company's quantity of qualified leads or ranking leads. Moreover, manually executing each program made it difficult to implement timely marketing campaigns. Because there was no system in place to identify each prospect's sales readiness, all leads went directly to the sales team. Three significant negative results of this were the waste of valuable time, the dilution of expensive resources, and the reduction of customer conversions.

SEO Schematics had never combined its customer and prospect databases, so its marketing department couldn't readily quantify campaign results in real terms of revenue. The department's records contained no demographics, and many other records were missing key pieces of information like email and mailing addresses and phone numbers, making additional contact difficult.

Unsure of which part of its marketing program most influenced its prospects' buying decisions, SEO Schematics had difficulty increasing the number of qualified leads at an acceptable cost. The company was poised to expand but has been held back by a lead-generation plateau and an inability to scale its marketing efforts to a wider audience while keeping costs-per-lead low.

The greatest challenges it faced were:

- Stagnant lead generation
- Poor lead differentiation
- Incomplete data capture
- Lack of ROI tracking
- Insufficient scalability

SEO Schematics' Marketing AI Process

Implementing the Marketing AI

After installing a MAS, SEO Schematics took the first step toward meeting its marketing challenges by building a Marketing AI to identify the components and processes responsible for driving successful sales. The system's reinforcement-learning capabilities make it responsive, allowing it to use actions — and feedback on the effects of those actions — to continuously improve marketing results. Installation isn't implementation, though, so the company worked with marketing automation specialists to design a comprehensive Marketing AI that everyone in the organization could use to improve their contributions to revenue generation. (See figure SEO S1)

SEO Schematics followed a simple, five-point plan based on a version of the Lead Lifecycle (Chapter 5) as its centerpiece:

1. **Discovery:** This step parallels the discovery phase of lead generation, revealing the information the company already has on its

leads and completing customer files using a streamlined set of data-governance rules.

2. **Attraction:** To earn more high-quality leads, SEO Schematics has to build more appeal into its content across all channels.

3. **Conversion:** Lead ranking and progress through the Lead Lifecycle ensures that no valuable leads are lost and that the sales team's energy isn't wasted on low-yield leads. Drip programs give every lead the right information at the right time.

4. **Closing:** The Lead Lifecycle carries prospects to the narrow end of the sales funnel, where the MAI synchronizes with the company's CRM system to maximize the sales team's ability to convert every highly qualified lead it receives into a sale.

5. **Analysis:** To improve future campaigns, the Marketing AI's analytics reveal who the company's customers are, where it can find more like them, and how it can deliver an even more successful nurture program to them next time.

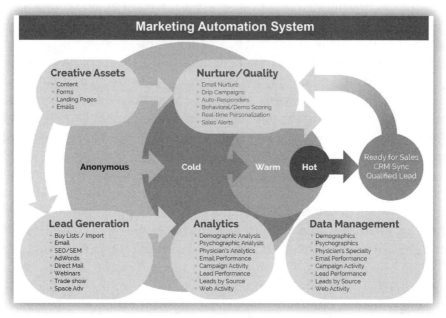

Figure SEO S1: Marketing Automation System

Phase 1: Discovery

Analyze and Profile Demographics
This phase begins with the receipt of all SEO Schematics customer and prospect files. Merging the files into one unduplicated database establishes a foundation for future data discovery and keeps records organized. Customer files get a "C" and prospect files get a "P" to differentiate them so that they can later follow different marketing flows based on their demographic, firmographic, behavioral, and contextual data.

Customer File Data Analysis
Customer file data analysis allows SEO Schematics to determine the influence each data element has on a prospect's inclination to make a purchase, which in turn affects lead score and progress along the marketing pipeline. The more data elements contained in a client's record, the more predictive this analysis will be. An analysis of the merged database (Table SEO S1) reveals insightful information.

SEO Schematics' unduplicated list contains 126,497 companies, but the file was missing important data elements. For example, only 67 percent of these companies had an email address, and only 68 percent had the contact's phone number. In addition, 19 percent lacked even a company's name, and 83 percent were at a business address. SEO Schematics' prospect records were even more likely than customers' records to lack important data elements. For example, 99 percent of the customer records had a postal address, while only 74 percent of the prospects did.

Presence of email address is an important indicator of the health of a list. With 79 percent of customers and 63 percent of prospects having an email address listed, these files had significant room for improvement. Another important point to note is the 16 percent of the file that contained home address records; only 35 percent of these had an email address. As you've learned, email is not only the most cost-effective method of communication, it's essential to a successful drip nurture campaign. The absence of an email address makes

Description	Total File		Has Postal Address		Has Business Address		Has Email Address		Has Phone numbers		Has Company Name	
	#	%	#	%	#	%	#	%	#	%	#	%
All Records	126,497	100%	118,491	94%	98,837	83%	84,882	67%	86,144	68%	102,543	81%
Customer Records	33,902	27%	33,697	99%	30,226	90%	26,918	79%	31,986	94%	32,351	95%
Prospect Records	92,595	73%	84,794	74%	68,611	81%	57,964	63%	54,158	58%	70,192	76%
Business Address	98,837	78%	98,837	83%	98,837	83%	74,549	75%	74,342	75%	96,876	98%
Consumer Address	19,654	16%	19,654	17%	-	0%	6,809	35%	7,320	37%	4,024	20%
No Postal Address	8,006	6%	-	0%	-	0%	3,524	44%	4,482	56%	1,643	21%
No Email Address	41,615	33%	33,609	83%	24,288	25%	0	0%	27,037	31%	27,012	26%

Table SEO S1: Customer File Data Element

closing a sale much less likely. Here's where the next implementation step comes in.

Data Append: Contact Information

To solve the problem of incomplete data, we match SEO Schematics' list against the ReachBase database that contains millions of records and append it with business-contact information, industry, and company size. Table SEO S2 shows the number of records appended and their impact on the file. In this case, the process appended 10,338 email addresses, an improvement of 38 percent.

Description	Records Appended				
	Total Records	Postal Address	Email Address	Phone Number	Company Name
All Records	13,727	3,365	10,338	11,077	12,372
Customer Records	4,181	44	3,918	1,801	3,218
Prospect Records	9,546	3,321	6,420	9,276	9,154
Postal Address	3,365	3,365	3,156	3,016	3,124
Email Address	10,338	3,156	10,338	9,635	9,587

Table SEO S2: Critical Contact Information Appended

Customer File Performance by Industry

Next, the SEO Schematics list needs firmographic data to go along with the newly complete customer and lead records. SIC industry codes identify and assign proper credit to each industry (Table SEO S3), giving SEO Schematics a far clearer picture of where its audience comes from and where its future efforts should go. In analyzing the data, we discovered that a prospect's industry type has a huge impact on its decision to purchase.

The MAS generates a market penetration score (MPS) for every record in the database by dividing the total number of customers and prospects by the total number of companies in its given industry. For example, SIC 73 (business services) produced the greatest number of customers and prospects, and it generated the highest MPS. The .38 percent score comes from dividing the number of customers the company already counted among its customer base, 5,625, by the 1,486,990 total companies in that industry. The MAI repeats this process for each

| Tier | SIC | Description | SEO Dynamics | | | | ReachBase | Market Penetration | |
			Customers	Prospects	Total	Close Rate	Companies	Customers	Prospects
1	73	BUSINESS SERVICES	5,625	14,342	19,967	0.28	1,486,990	0.38%	0.96%
1	27	PRINTING, PUBLISHING	893	2,584	3,477	0.26	246,483	0.36%	1.05%
1	70	HOTELS AND LODGING	623	1,495	2,118	0.29	172,317	0.36%	0.87%
1	82	EDUCATIONAL SERVICES	1,625	11,284	12,909	0.13	750,782	0.22%	1.50%
1	87	ENG, ACCTG, MGMT	2,364	7,126	9,490	0.25	1,166,752	0.20%	0.61%
1	63	INSURANCE CARRIERS	424	2,756	3,180	0.13	215,055	0.20%	1.28%
1	81	LEGAL SERVICES	1,286	3,079	4,365	0.29	654,300	0.20%	0.47%
1	64	INSURANCE AGENTS	459	1,237	1,696	0.27	392,504	0.12%	0.32%
1	57	FURNITURE STORES	402	1,395	1,797	0.22	351,925	0.11%	0.40%
1	65	REAL ESTATE	771	1,718	2,489	0.31	786,872	0.10%	0.22%
1	Total		14,472	47,016	61,488	0.24	6,223,980	0.23%	0.76%
2	50	WHOLESALE DURABLE	732	1,849	2,581	0.28	757,197	0.10%	0.24%
2	52	BLDG MATRLS, HRDWR	196	387	583	0.34	207,673	0.09%	0.19%
2	58	RESTAURANTS & BARS	745	1,050	1,795	0.42	802,154	0.09%	0.13%
2	48	COMMUNICATIONS	175	872	1,047	0.17	223,279	0.08%	0.39%
2	56	APPAREL & ACCESSORY	167	357	524	0.32	213,709	0.08%	0.17%
2	25	FURNITURE & FIXTURES	26	102	128	0.20	35,369	0.07%	0.29%
2	72	PERSONAL SERVICES	467	734	1,201	0.39	815,840	0.06%	0.09%
2	80	HEALTH SERVICES	934	4,851	5,785	0.16	1,830,612	0.05%	0.26%
2	53	GENERAL MERCH	54	406	460	0.12	107,187	0.05%	0.38%
2	17	CONSTRUCT-SPECIAL	495	914	1,409	0.35	1,117,054	0.04%	0.08%
2	Total		3,991	11,522	15,513	0.26	6,110,074	0.07%	0.19%

Table SEO S3: Customer File Analysis: Appended Industries

industry and ranks each customer and prospect industry in descending order of importance.

Next, (Table SEO S4) we group industries together by assigning them to one of five performance tiers, based on their market penetration index.

Tier	% of Customer	Industry Profile	SEO Dynamics Appended			ReachBase Companies	Market Penetration	
			Customers	Prospects	Total		Customers	Prospects
1	74%	Top 10 Industries	14,472	47,016	61,488	6,223,980	0.233%	0.755%
2	20%	Next 10 Industries	3,991	11,522	15,513	6,110,074	0.065%	0.189%
3	3%	Next 10 Industries	625	2,813	3,438	2,502,087	0.025%	0.112%
4	2%	Next 20 Industries	332	1,980	2,312	2,115,732	0.016%	0.094%
5	1%	Next 20 Industries	190	1,174	1,364	4,235,247	0.004%	0.028%
Total	100%	80 Industries	19,610	64,505	84,115	21,187,120	0.093%	0.304%

Table SEO S4: Customer File Analysis: Appended Industry Tier Summary

The first tier comprising the top 10 industries generated 74 percent of the customers, while the bottom tier comprising 20 industries generated only 1 percent of the customers. All industries had an equal opportunity to respond to SEO Schematics' marketing. Therefore, according to the analysis, companies in the top industry tier were *74 times more likely* to make a purchase than the bottom tier. That's a huge drop-off in ROI, and it instantly allows SEO Schematics to trim its marketing budget by narrowing the firm's marketing focus to the industries that make up the bulk of its business.

Another important indicator of marketing success is the close rate, the percentage of prospects that convert into customers. Table SEO S5 indicates

Tier	% of Customers	Profile	SEO Dynamics Appended			
			Customers	Prospects	Total	Close Rate
1	74%	Top 10 Industries	14,472	47,016	61,488	0.235
2	20%	Next 10 Industries	3,991	11,522	15,513	0.257
3	3%	Next 10 Industries	625	2,813	3,438	0.182
4	2%	Next 20 Industries	332	1,980	2,312	0.143
5	1%	Next 20 Industries	190	1,174	1,364	0.139
Total	100%	80 Industries	19,610	64,505	84,115	0.233

Table SEO S5: Customer File Analysis: Industry Close Rate Summary

that closing a sale on a lead in the top industry tier is nearly 2 times as likely as the bottom tier. Sending leads in tier five to the sales team is clearly a waste of SEO Schematics' resources, and the Marketing AI highlights that wasted effort so it can be rechanneled in more profitable directions.

Customer File Performance by Job Title and Company Size

Last, the MAI team examines the job title and company's employee-size information appended to SEO Schematics' list to determine if these data

Data File	Job Title	Company's Employee Size						Total
		1-25	26-99	100-499	500-999	1000+	Unknown	
S E O S C H E M A T I C S	Corporate Mgmt	741	539	43	19	-	956	2,299
	IT	8	353	1,355	802	602	1,068	4,187
	Sales & Marketing	1,748	3,934	2,343	890	1,876	1,906	12,697
	Other	1,686	1,525	2,326	1,040	1,035	7,107	14,421
	Total - All Job Titles	4,183	6,351	6,067	2,751	3,513	11,037	33,902
R E A C H B A S E	Corporate Mgmt	5,648,541	1,839,451	325,516	90,360	180,994	1,757,381	9,842,243
	IT	732,316	749,968	516,051	200,855	626,350	482,418	3,307,958
	Sales & Marketing	866,532	1,157,644	481,548	165,588	441,673	461,125	3,574,110
	Other	16,475,721	8,617,858	3,255,460	973,460	3,214,005	8,998,736	41,535,240
	Total - All Job Titles	23,723,110	12,364,921	4,578,575	1,430,263	4,463,022	11,699,660	58,259,551
P E N E T R A T I O N	Corporate Mgmt	0.01%	0.03%	0.01%	0.02%	0.00%	0.05%	0.02%
	IT	0.00%	0.05%	0.26%	0.40%	0.10%	0.22%	0.13%
	Sales & Marketing	0.20%	0.34%	0.49%	0.54%	0.42%	0.41%	0.36%
	Other	0.01%	0.02%	0.07%	0.11%	0.03%	0.08%	0.03%
	Total - All Job Titles	0.02%	0.05%	0.13%	0.19%	0.08%	0.09%	0.06%

Table SEO S6: Customer File Summary: Job Title and Company-Size Analysis

elements have an impact on the customer's tendency to buy. The results, summarized in Table SEO S6, reveal that a marketing strategy focused on sales, marketing and information technology job titles were 10 times more likely to make a purchase. In addition, companies with 100 to 999 employees were two to three times more likely to buy. Company size and job title are both important factors in customer activity, and the MAI also learns to apply this information to lead scoring.

Conclusion: Customer File Data Analysis

The append analysis concluded that all future marketing decisions for SEO Schematics should be guided by a combination of industry, address, job title and company size filters to increase the effectiveness of future sales and marketing campaigns.

Phase 2: Attraction

The next step in the process is to identify all marketing channels, tradeshows, and other industry sources that serve to target and attract the decision-making executives who have the job titles, industries, and company sizes identified as top performers in the Discovery phase. Importantly, the MAI tags costs for each lead and source are attached to each record on the database, so ROI can be verified throughout the Lead Lifecycle.

Postal and Email Lists: We added 36 third-party email and postal lists (comprising marketing, IT, and corporate management lists) to the MAI's marketing database. Email links received tags with the medium and program name for respondents; direct mail respondents got tagged with personal URLs (PURL).

Trade Shows: SEO Schematics historically had exhibited at 12 marketing trade shows. The MAS compared the customer-file data analysis against the attendee profiles from each trade show to identify the industry, job title, and company size profiles that best matched the company's target market as defined by the data gathered in the Discovery phase. Based on the analysis, the original dozen shows were reduced to five, and one new show that had promising attendee records was added.

The way SEO Schematics handles its trade shows needs thought to garner more engagement and collect more valuable data. The MAI will now track attendee badges as they're scanned at the trade shows, and the company also plans to hold raffles for iPads and other prizes to earn business-card information from raffle participants. After gathering these names, they're added to the company's MAI and tagged with the trade show attended, along with the cost to exhibit at each show:

- Tradeshow A – $20,000
- Tradeshow B – $35,000
- Tradeshow C – $10,000
- Tradeshow D – $15,000
- Tradeshow E – $45,000
- Tradeshow F – $12,000

SEO, SEM, and Social Marketing: The leads that organic and paid searches bring in are some of the easiest to track for essential behavioral and contextual data. To take advantage of online leads, the MAI specialists divide paid, organic, and social sources by platform, keyword, and referrer:

- Paid search (SEM) on Bing, Google, Yahoo, and other relevant search engines were tagged based on word searched.
- Organic search (SEO) on the major search engines were tagged based on referrer.
- Social platforms, including Facebook, LinkedIn, and Twitter, received referrer tags.
- Referring websites that linked to SEO Schematics, including blogs and industry journals, also got referrer tags.
- Other sources, including direct visits and https:// referrals were tagged as "Direct." Because these visitors had sufficient interest to seek out the site directly, they're of particular note.

Content: SEO Schematics must prioritize content and match it to Lead Lifecycle stages, because content is the fuel that propels leads through the sales pipeline. Also, because the firm's clients expect the company that serves them SEO software solutions to maintain top-quality content, it's even more vital to get this phase of Marketing AI implementation right. To bring SEO Schematics' content up to the high standards its clientele expects, we made the following three changes:

1. Rewriting sections of SEO Schematics' website to supply custom content for each of the company's target audiences — in this case, sales, marketing, and IT, the three industries pinpointed during Discovery. The Marketing AI delivers customized content to visitors based on data that is continuously updated. This means the need for frequent updates to the site is imperative.

2. Adding a blog with custom-crafted content for each of the three buyer categories. Each blog post also gets its own tags to make finding similar articles easier for visitors, thus enhancing the value of the blog as a reference library with each new article posted.

3. Developing white papers, feature-length articles, and e-books for drip campaigns that meet the needs of leads at every phase of the Lead Lifecycle. By dividing content according to whether it's meant for leads at the top, middle, or bottom of the funnel, SEO Schematics is ready to supply leads' needs at every step of its buyers' journeys.

Phase 3: Conversion

Here's where the Lead Lifecycle swings into action. It allows the MAI team to organize customer data, content channels, and behavioral information into a lead scoring system that maximizes the value of every lead according to engagement and source.

Nurture Programs

At the heart of SEO Schematics' marketing overhaul is the establishment of nurture programs that allow leads to flow effortlessly through the marketing pipeline, getting all the information the company needs to make informed buying decisions. Nurture campaigns that use collected data to predict what prospects will need as they need it address the company's scalability challenge, allowing it to know precisely how much marketing spend it will need to bring in a reliable number of qualified leads.

The newly unveiled SEO Schematics nurture program comprises multiple flows, all of which make email a central component. Ongoing communication with promising leads is key, and email is the most cost-effective way of reaching the larger audiences the company now has. Its new-to-file nurture campaigns are further divided by job function into the three high-value categories identified earlier, sales, marketing, and information technology executives.

Lead Scoring

SEO Schematics' Marketing AI system initially scores each prospect's likelihood of conversion based on demographic profiles, then on firmographic data. It further categorizes leads based on behavioral and contextual data as this information comes in, all of which it continues to learn about and adjust over time. Lead scores change over time and govern the directions leads take through the marketing pipeline. They also synch with the customized Lead Lifecycle program.

New leads go through a demographic gate to identify traffic that is not a lead so that these results can be dead-ended. For leads that do qualify, the system assigns them to the appropriate place on the Lead Lifecycle.

A solid lead scoring system eliminates the company's problem with lead generation and differentiation, ensuring that the sales team only gets properly qualified leads. By synching MAS and CRM data regularly, the hand-off from marketing to sales is seamless. The initial SEO Schematics lead scoring strategy assigns higher weight to the three key industries that comprise most of the company's business, but crucially, the scoring system itself adapts to changes. If the system notes a surge in manufacturing-engineering companies, it can be taught to weigh this sector more highly and to develop a new content stream to meet the needs of this emerging market.

Real-Time Personalization

By using a nurturing program score and scripting to trigger delivery of RTP marketing content, SEO Schematics is able to educate leads and accelerate the progression from prospect to customer. Triggered delivery and guided content are part of what distinguishes automated marketing from conventional tactics, and are a cornerstone of the new SEO Schematics strategy. For SEO Schematics, being able to quantify a leads' sales readiness dramatically increases returns on the company's time invested. SEO Schematics' nurturing program scores now become the foundation for developing useful scripts to guide its prospects' flow through the sales pipeline. Instead of guessing when its customers need information, the company's new nurture program supplies information on demand, ensuring the right people get the right message at the right time.

SEO also has an online marketing-preference center that provides prospects and customers with the ability to designate their preferred method and frequency of contact. Opting down is always preferable to opting out, and customers prefer to set the tone of their interactions with companies. SEO Schematics can also use information gathered from preference pages to further educate its Marketing AI about its customer base.

Phase 4: Closing

SEO Schematics' MAS integrates its scoring system with the company's CRM system and prioritizes a prospect's readiness for a sales call. When the prospect exceeds a predictive score, the Marketing AI triggers a timely alert to the sales team. Then the sales team concentrates only on leads that are fully sales-qualified and ready to buy, resulting in a substantial increase in conversion rates.

Phase 5: Analytics

SEO Schematics implemented campaign analytics to determine the most cost effective combination of marketing content, tactics and channels to increase the number of customers for each dollar spent. The power of analytics lies in addition by subtraction. SEO Schematics can use data gleaned from analytics to go from conventional marketing to *revenue performance marketing* by zooming in on high-ROI actions. By jettisoning the parts of their marketing strategy that no longer work, the firm gains a better understanding of what gives results.

SEO Schematics' marketing automation platform produces a series of reports detailing results of the solution quantifying the scalability, predictability, reproducibility, and success of the the company's marketing program. Clear, concise reports are SEO Schematics' road map to future success, making each iteration of its Marketing AI campaigns able to deliver more well-nurtured prospects, more highly qualified leads, and ultimately, more revenue. Their key reports include:

- ✓ **Source Attribution:** SEO Schematics' Marketing AI is connected to its automation system that attributes influence and effectiveness of each advertising campaign on a prospect's decision to purchase. The system provides reports that clearly show the value of the different sources that populated SEO's database.
- ✓ **First Touch and Multi-touch Sales Attribution:** Attributions also go to successive sources, not a single source, for a more nuanced view of where the company's marketing strategies are truly enjoying their most significant successes.
- ✓ **Behavioral Data:** After noting behavioral data from customers that move through the marketing pipeline, it's possible to assign weight to various behaviors and demographic details. For example, SEO Schematics noted that visitors who search on a specific keyword or downloaded a particular white paper had a phenomenal 60 percent conversion rate, making this action a strong signal of sales readiness. The system weights this action significantly, according it a higher value than actions that carry weaker signals. By prioritizing behaviors, the system identifies the key elements of future effective nurture programs.
- ✓ **ROI:** The system has earmarked costs and revenue returns on every aspect of a marketing campaign, making it possible to track ROI accurately across all channels and for all leads.

✓ **Lead and Customer Profiling:** SEO Schematics' Marketing AI continuously analyzes and profiles the demographics of customers to determine the sales-lead characteristics that predict those most likely to buy. When the company understands its current customers thoroughly, it can readily find more like them. Demographic, firmographic, behavioral, and contextual data go into this comprehensive analysis.

Marketing Challenge Resolved

By implementing a MAS that works with the marketing team's AI experts and that synchs with the CRM system for a seamless transition to sales, SEO Schematics has successfully addressed all its challenges.

1. **Stagnant lead generation** — Refocusing marketing efforts on high-value industries, adding new lists, cleansing the house list, and nurturing every prospect with customized drip programs have led to a boom in new, qualified leads.
2. **Poor lead differentiation** — The company's new lead scoring program prepares every lead for the transition to sales. Each lead has a more complete file thanks to data append processes and better audience segmentation.
3. **Incomplete data capture** — Marketing automation, data append, cross-referencing with a larger data file, and implementing new marketing techniques have led to a significant increase in data capture rates, which in turn leads to better nurture campaigns and customization.
4. **Lack of ROI tracking** — The cost of each lead and that lead's expected value is now quantifiable. Conventional marketing has become revenue marketing in earnest with a Marketing AI.
5. **Insufficient scalability** — SEO Schematics is ready to grow with its new and deeper understanding of its customer base, influx of highly qualified leads, and ready recognition of emerging markets.

Epilogue

T oday, Marketing AI has moved beyond the confines of the laboratory into the new digital world, where a complete, intelligent, integrated process unifies the symbiosis between sales and marketing. Marketing AI has opened a new realm of possibilities. Companies communicate with prospects and customers based on the context in which they operate. It functions in every phase of the marketing cycle, from discovery to execution and analysis. It brings together every aspect of your marketing efforts into one cohesive force that adapts and responds from beginning to end.

The speed at which your prospects move through your lead life cycle dictates how many sales you make. Having the capability to scan the entirety of your market and get your audience to interact with you holds the key to your organization's future.

In today's world of highly evolved marketing, it's not enough to have astounding creative or mountains of data in isolation. You need a Marketing AI that sees where your traffic is really coming from and how to control and profit from it. Your MAI gives you greater predictability of everything from lead acquisition and lead nurturing to customer retention. Predictability combined with scalability and reproducibility is the key to sustaining the growth and success of your company. And because marketing automation is a nascent technology, you have plenty of choices between systems right now; but no matter which one you choose, installation isn't the same as implementation. To make the most of any software, you need to understand its capabilities and the environment in which it operates.

Throughout *Marketing AI: From Automation to Revenue Performance Marketing*, you've learned how marketing automation works within the context of traditional marketing. It's that fusion of art and science that transforms automation into AI. The DNA of your existing customer base extends far beyond demographics and behavioral scores. Developing a deep, thorough understanding of how your customers interact with you closely correlates with sales now and into the future.

In our Prologue we discussed whether Marketing AI passes the Turing Test, a test that requires a computer to deceive a human being that it's human. In other words, can the Marketing AI that exists today learn, grow, adapt, and respond as a human mind does? The answer is, unequivocally, yes. MAI does possess the ability to act in the way the human mind does, and that ability provides unmistakable advantages for humans.

No individual part of a conventional marketing strategy — no data governance plan, no campaign execution blueprint, no degree of cooperation between marketing and sales — can match what a Marketing AI can coordinate for you. Coordinating a complex, omni-channel marketing strategy by hand would be an impossible task for a human. Marketing AI doesn't just deliver better results; it's critical to providing the complete, customized user experience that sets you apart in a world that demands your attention.

Marketing has always had intelligent control, but until technology caught up, it was strictly human intelligence. An immense amount of thought and planning goes into building a brand, creating buzz, nurturing leads, and preparing future customers for the hand-off to the sales team. The industry has become so sophisticated, though, that a single marketing mind — or even a well-coordinated team — can't track every campaign, every channel, every customer with the precise timing and customized content that's needed to set businesses apart from the pack.

Enter automation. With marketing automation, you turn the art of marketing into a science and give it the steady, quantifiable metrics that make every action you take easier to manage and every action that your leads take simpler to track. It's a powerful tool for amplifying your marketing team's brightest ideas and for freeing it to focus on creative while your automation software handles the execution.

Marketing automation is far more than just a way to automate the details: Marketing automation systems learn from past campaigns, reveal where your best leads are, coordinate cross-channel marketing campaigns with a few clicks, and develop flows to nurture those leads as they move through your marketing pipeline. It places demographic, firmographic, and behavioral data into a contextual framework that lets you deliver precisely the right information at just the right time.

Marketing AI promotes more satisfied customers, which translates into more repeat purchases because customers have better buying experiences. The marketing journey each customer takes is unique, but with your Marketing AI your leads no longer take their journeys in isolation. Now you're able to guide them every step of the way.